Presented to

_____

_____

_____

_____

_____

_____

_____

THE APOSTOLIC CHURCH

ONE, HOLY, CATHOLIC AND MISSIONARY

ROBERT J. SCUDIERI

LUTHERAN SOCIETY FOR MISSIOLOGY
BOOK SERIES

EUGENE W. BUNKOWSKE
SERIES EDITOR

ERWIN J. KOLB & DANIEL N. HARMELINK
ASSISTING EDITORS

1996

Scudieri, Robert J. *The Apostolic Church: One, Holy, Catholic and Missionary.* The Lutheran Society for Missiology Book Series. Forward by Won Yong Ji. Eugene W. Bunkowske, Series Editor. Erwin J. Kolb and Daniel N. Harmelink, Assisting Editors. Lutheran Society for Missiology, 1996 (includes endnotes and index).

For more information regarding the Lutheran Society for Missiology and other publications available from the Lutheran Society for Missiology Book Series, please write or telephone:

> Rev. Dr. Eugene W. Bunkowske
> Concordia Theological Seminary
> 6600 North Clinton Street
> Fort Wayne, IN 46825-4996 USA
>
> > TEL 219/452-2173
> > FAX 219/452-2121

ISBN 0-9648764-0-X

Contents

Series Introduction

The purpose of the *Lutheran Society for Missiology Book Series* otherwise known as *Lutheran Mission Books* is to make available to the Christian community missiological material and resources which are clearly from a Lutheran perspective, resources that are not available from any other source. This series also seeks to encourage scholars to develop and write books from a Lutheran mission perspective that would not be published and distributed by a larger publisher.

The *Lutheran Mission Books Series* is published by the Lutheran Society for Missiology with a worldwide membership of over two hundred people. This new society is not only growing internationally but also regionally with local chapters organized in major centers such as Ft. Wayne, Indiana; Gary, Indiana; St. Louis, Missouri and St. Paul\Minneapolis, Minnesota. The formation of additional chapters in the United States and in other countries of the world is in progress at this time.

The society was formed to give Lutheran Christians an opportunity to boldly and courageously communicate their Apostolic roots. The LSfM stands for God's Biblical Mission in action. It stands for the fact that the mission of "seeking and saving the lost" was, and still is, God's mission and that Lutherans together with all other believes in Jesus Christ are God's chosen means for getting the "means of grace" to a lost and dying world. The Lutheran Society for Missiology is dedicated to the fact that Dr. Martin Luther and those who stand in his line are totally committed to the proclamation of the true Word of God as expressed in the Lutheran Confessions in practical ways that reach the hearts and minds of the common person, no matter what his or her language and cultural background, without regard to social status or wealth.

The Lutheran Society for Missiology is a freestanding organization with its own distinct agendas. Recognizing that mission boards and independent mission sending agencies need a "think tank" component to move them forward in God's mission today, the LSfM has keyed-in on the task of providing the theological and theoretical underpinning for understanding and doing God's mission. The LSfM is committed to doing this theological and theoretical work in ways that also suggest the appropriate kind of practical applications in a variety of social and cultural contexts. Its basic purpose is to explore the Biblical relatedness of mission theology and application. The LSfM believes that "the best mission theory makes for the best mission practice."

The future will see the Lutheran Society for Missiology creatively developing its thinking and growing in Triune God-centered Biblical mission. Regular meetings will continue to bring mission-minded Lutherans together in ways that generate mission thinking and actions. It is our prayer that the number of LSfM members will increase markedly and that the multiplication of local chapters in the United States and worldwide will make a significant contribution to what the LSfM is and does. It is also our prayer that missiology from a Biblical and Lutheran Confessional perspective will develop through the study and experience of the LSfM and its individual members and that the LSfM journal *Missio Apostolica* will be supplemented with the publication of mission books (of which *The Apostolic Church* is the first) and the LSfM *Communicator* which will soon be available to the LSfM membership on a regular basis. As the strength of the Lutheran Society for Missiology under God increases, the area of audio and video materials will also come forward and become more and more pivotal.

As the LSfM moves into its God-ordained future, it will be a continual meeting place for mission minded people. God has already chosen these people to be significant participants on His mission team. As a team, these people will, in the years and decades to come, carry out under God's direction and power his worldwide mission of reaching the lost and nurturing the found with His Word and the Sacraments.

To God be the glory for what He has done and will continue to do through the Lutheran Society for Missiology.

Rev. Eugene W. Bunkowske, Ph.D., Litt. D., D.D.
Lutheran Society for Missiology Book Series
Series Editor and Graduate Professor of Missions
Concordia Theological Seminary, Ft. Wayne, Indiana

Foreword

Dr. Robert Scudieri has ventured out on an interesting but not an easy excursion on the original meaning of *the Apostolic Church* as expressed in the Nicene Creed. It is to discover the true Biblical meaning and historical meaning of the word *apostolic* being used with the Church. He contends that the rapid "growth" of the church should be explained by theological substance of the church rather than by modern sociology and pop-psychology, frequently the case in our days. The Church is by nature *missionary*; it has unmistakably a missionary character. Scudieri is seriously endeavoring to find a new, realistic and viable paradigm that is historically, theologically and Biblically sound, a paradigm applicable and practical for now and in the years to come.

What will the twenty-first century bring for the Christian Mission? The ultimate concern of Mission may be the same, yet the mission enterprise will be a different ballgame with new rules and new kinds of contenders; opponents who will shake-up the very foundations of the Judeo-Christian traditions in the West. A noticeable challenger, for example, is the new age mode of thinking—a gnosticism of our time and an unprecedented grand syncretism. How will the Church cope with the complicated/complex/inclusive phenomena in the area of "religions" and witness Christ and his saving Gospel to a peculiarly secularized generation is one of the challenging tasks of all Christian theologians, missiologists, mission executives, strategists and missionaries. Both syncretism and universalism are all around us. No less than a "full armor of God" is called for (1Pet 3:15, Eph 6:10-17). Mission must turn its attention to a new direction by developing more convincing arguments against the challenges and threats posed by various spiritualities. These include the Stoic pantheism of the East (a naturalistic *Weltanschauung*), the Epicurean "successism" of the West and many explicit and implicit movements of internationalism, localism, ethnocentrism, nationalism, multiculturalism and the general trend of contextualization of religion. Such a confusing scene today is the very context in which the unchanging Text of the Gospel has to be packaged and presented meaningfully and relevantly without distorting its salvific content.

It appears to be the strong contention of the author that the true and correct meaning of the *apostolic church* in history—the *missionary church*—

may lead us to the right answers. Furthermore, it can be a correct perception of missions and the realistically conceivable *Anknüpfungspunkt* (a point of contact, a point of departure) of the theory and the practice of Christian missions without unnecessary conflict. Again, the apostolic nature of the New Testament Church has a distinct missionary character. The reader may observe the author's answers and suggestions for resolving the tension. Will sociology, applied psychology, pop-philosophy, cultural anthropology, etc. provide answers to the tough issues and problems related to Christian missions in this post-modern era? No, Scudieri is sceptical about drawing such conclusions. They may give some assistance, if properly utilized without watering down the real substance of the Gospel of Christ and its witness; nevertheless, they cannot possibly offer the ultimate solution and answer.

This monograph is a dedicated search for the origin of the creedal statement, *apostolic church* with an inherent missionary emphasis. The church above all is an apostolic or missionary church. The word *apostolic* should be understood from the point of "sentness." The author traces the meaning back in the history of the early New Testament Church. It provides significant portion of the history of theology.

From this point of view, the monograph may enlighten the reader on the nature of the church, first of all, and presents a considerable number of new insights into the meaning of *apostle* and being *apostolic*. The author himself takes very seriously this privilege of "sentness" to North America and elsewhere. One may find all these by reading though this unique undertaking.

Is an interesting step forward in search of another new dimension of the real "nature" the church which may positively strengthen the life of the church and its witness to Jesus Christ. It also clarifies the true identity of the church. At any rate, the result of his deliberation will give much or thought— something to think about! May this search go forward.

Indeed, it is very appropriate in my estimation to publish this intense search for God's mission for/to the world as the first volume of this *Lutheran Society for Missiology Book Series*. Furthermore, the expertise of the series and assisting editors has added further clarification to the succinct analysis of the author. I highly recommend the text that follows to all those who are vitally interested in missions. Read his words, study his ideas and reflect on the challenge which he presents in his work. One may obtain much profitable knowledge and experience.

Rev. Dr. Won Yong Ji
Professor of Systematic Theology
Concordia Seminary, St. Louis, Missouri

Dedication

This work is dedicated to the most supportive, loving and patient family any one person could have. My wife, Lynn, my children, Nathan and Alison, have endured my times away to work on this manuscript with grace and love. In large part they are responsible for this book.

Prologue
The Search Begins

On January 3, 1991 I began a journey to Rome, Constantinople and Nicea without ever having left the Overseas Ministries Study Center in New Haven, Connecticut. On a six month study leave I had three specific goals:

1. To search for the origin of the term *apostolic church*.
2. To examine the missionary emphasis inherent in that term.
3. To give the church a new vantage point from which to see the significance of these important words.

Few will deny that the church of the first three centuries grew rapidly. By the end of the first century there were Christian churches all over the Mediterranean world. Many historians, however, explain this rapid growth with natural sociological and historical causes. I believe we should instead look for the reasons for church growth in the heart of the church, and, according to the Nicene Creed, one facet of that heart is apostolic.

While the term *apostolic church* is not in the Bible, the concept certainly is. For example, St. Paul makes it clear to the Ephesian Christians as to who they really are:

> Consequently, you are no longer foreigners and aliens, but fellow citizens with God's people and members of God's household, built on the foundation of the apostles and prophets, with Christ Jesus himself as the chief cornerstone. (Eph 2:19-20)

In order to understand how the early Christians understood the term *apostolic church* as it is used in the Nicene Creed, it is necessary to take a little tour of early church history. This kind of exploration is exciting, because through it we can learn more about the sending (apostolic) nature of God himself! (Jn 17:4, 18)

Early Christians understood themselves to be the covenant people of God—charged with the task of witnessing to all nations. It was not long before this initially frightened group of men and women were planting churches all over the known world. In other words, early Christians knew they were a missionary people. They learned this from the Apostles them-

1

selves who were taught and sent by Christ (Acts 1:7, 8; Acts 4; Acts 8:4, *et alia*).

The first apostles were chosen by Jesus. St. Paul was an *apostle,* a "sent one," but chosen later, "as one born out of due time." In 1 Corinthians 12:29 he implies that the office of apostle was not for everyone. The Apostles were a distinct, select group of sent ones instructed by Christ to spread the Gospel. Christians today are not Apostles, but the "sentness" aspect of apostleship is incumbent on every Christian —hence the apostolic character of the new testament church.

The adjective *apostolic* is a word English speaking people have borrowed from the Greeks. It is a verbal adjective, taken from the verb *apostellein,* which means "to send out." The noun is *apostle* (Greek: *apostolos*). In usage this word is predominantly passive in character, "to be sent."

The first appearance of the adjective *apostolic* in Christian writing is not all that auspicious. Around AD 110 the Christian bishop Ignatius was being led to his death by a troop of Roman soldiers. On the way to his final witness this old faithful leader of the early church thought first of others. Along the route to his execution he wrote a series of letters to congregations, to console and encourage *them.* In the letter to the Tralleans Ignatius made the claim that he was writing "after the apostolic manner," that is, "as the apostles wrote."

In the New Testament the first apostles were those chosen by Jesus to expand his work of bringing the Good News of God's gift of salvation to all. The noun is common in the New Testament but the adjective *apostolic* is not normally used in the church until the third and fourth centuries, and then it described certain writings of the apostles, particularly Scripture.

Apostolic is a word that connects us to the church of all times, but especially to the church of the New Testament. We naturally relate *apostolic* to The Twelve apostles. It feels as if it were a first century expression, and we appreciate the continuity with the Twelve. The New Testament connection is certainly important, especially if we understand the passive implication of apostolic, that we too are sent to be witnesses. Yet this important term has been given different accents over the last twenty centuries.

Sometimes those who say the church is apostolic are describing its doctrine. George Forell, a noted Lutheran theologian, gives this definition:

> When we confess our faith in the "apostolic church" we are *setting limits* [emphasis mine] to the religious discussion. The [Nicene] Creed defines the faith of the Christian church as "apostolic". This means that Christianity is based on the witness of the apostles as we find it in the Bible. This apostolic witness defines and limits the Christian message. It is the standard by which it must be measured.[1]

Frankly, I believe this understanding, though certainly true, is too narrow; something very important is left out.

That "something" is the mission activity of the Apostles. When we call the church apostolic we are talking about more than just our pedigree; we are declaring the church's missionary task. Of course apostolic means that the church continues to believe the *doctrine* of the first apostles. But it means something more. It means that the church continues to *do* what the apostles did, because the church also has been sent by the same Sender, (Mt 24:14).

I particularly appreciate the insight of Bible scholar T.W. Manson. He says,

> It is a pity that the word "apostolic" has had its meaning narrowed in the course of the centuries, so that instead of declaring primarily the church's commitment to a great missionary task, it merely registers a claim on the part of the Eastern and Roman Communions to be lawful successors of the apostles.[2]

Why has it been so hard for the church to hold on to its missionary character? At the outset the church could not be contained. In the next chapter I will show how the desire of those first believers to tell the Gospel pushed the borders of the unevangelized world back further and further. As a result by the second century many thought the entire known world embraced the love of Christ.

But in later centuries the Bride of Christ, his church, acted as if mission work were an elective and not a binding commitment. George Vicedom complained that "God has had to wring missionary commitment from his church."[3]

The tendency was for the church to limit her mission to holding onto doctrine, reaffirming for herself the basics of the faith and cultivating a comfortable fellowship of believers. Paul complained to the Hebrew Christians (Heb 6:1, 10) that it was time to move past the teaching of the basics, and move on to more mature activities. Is it necessary to lay a foundation over and over again before the structure is built?

An apostolic church is one that is on the move, going to where it has not gone before. When Jesus installed the first twelve as apostles they had two responsibilities: "—that they might be with him and that he might send them out to preach ..." (Mk 3:14).

Matthew said that the apostles were to go out to make disciples, by baptizing and teaching (Mt 28:18-20). Luke declared that the apostles were to preach repentance and forgiveness in Christ's name to all nations (Lk 24:44-46). In John the resurrected Christ appeared to his disciples and told them "As the Father has sent me, I am sending you." (Jn 20:21) Christ sends the eleven in that room as his apostles, his sent ones and gives them the power to

declare the forgiveness of sins (21:23). That power of the keys and that sentness by implication is intended for all believers, for the priesthood of believers, the church. The church is thus apostolic.

To be in continuity with the apostles is to be sent out.

It is my conviction that today more than ever churches must move outside
of their boundaries. There are approximately 5.6 billion people alive on this
planet. One third of them, about 1.9 billion are Christians. About one billion
non-Christians live next door to those Christians and have easy access to the
Gospel. But one half of the world, two and a half billion human beings, will
not be reached if no concerted effort is made to bring them the Good News.
We have been sent—we are on a mission to bring the Gospel to all people.

The church must move outside of herself. This is not her doing but God's.
As the Willingen Conference affirmed, the missionary mandate "has its source
in the Triune God himself." The One who carried our failures to a cross
intends to carry his message to the world. God will not be deterred and cannot
be thwarted. The question really is "Who of us will be there with God?"

How will we describe the church in these last days of the twentieth century? By numbers? By doctrines? By what she does? The Nicene Creed tell
us about the character of the church. The word *apostolic* includes the meaning missionary. Each time we confess this Creed we are really saying the
church is missionary.

I began my research for the meaning of the phrase *apostolic church* in
Nicea, a small town about thirty miles south of the old Roman capital of
Nicomedia. I wanted to know what the Council of Nicea, convened in AD
325, meant when it called the church *apostolic*.

My first shock was to find out that the word was not in the creed adopted
at Nicea. Later I will describe how it was added to the Creed and became a
synonym for orthodoxy, correct teaching. But it does not have that meaning
everywhere in the fourth century. By rummaging around in those old hall-
ways I was able to discover ancient clues to help a modern people rediscover
lost pieces of their past. Some of those discoveries sent me further back in
time, back to the apostles themselves!

I followed the trail of *apostolic church* to the system of apostles used by
the Jews since the time of Chronicles, and then to the other apostles named in
the New Testament (those besides The Twelve mentioned in Scripture) and
right up through missionary work in the second and third century. In all these
periods apostolic carries the connotation of missionary.

To begin then, we go first to the seldom visited regions of the Jewish apostle.

Part I
"The one sent by a man
is as the man himself."
—an old rabbinic saying

The Jews were a significant part of the landscape of the Roman Empire. The total population of the empire under Caesar Augustus was about fifty-four million; of this figure approximately seven percent, four and a half million, were Jewish. In 5 BC there were approximately ten thousand Jews living in Rome. Jews of Jesus' day had strong political influence and were socially prominent. By bringing large numbers of pagans under their influence they had grown in importance—and that growth looked as if it were going to continue.

To stay in touch with Jewish settlements throughout the world, Jews developed an infrastructure that allowed the leadership in Jerusalem to transmit messages whenever there was a need—an early "Pony Express," without the horses. They devised a system of authorized messengers to provide oversight for those far away from Jerusalem. This was an essential part of the growth of Judaism, a growth that is much greater than we realize.

Chapter 1
The Jewish Mission

Unlike today, the Jews of Jesus' time saw mission work as a duty. The apostle Paul sums up just how important it was for Jews to share their faith: the Jew understood himself to be

> a guide for the blind, a light for those who are in the dark, an instructor of the foolish, a teacher of infants, because you have in the law the embodiment of knowledge and truth ... (Rom 2:19-20).

Jews knew they had something unique to say to the world, something which was important to every person: that there is only one God, the One who created heaven and earth, and who had revealed his will in the form of the Torah, the Holy Law. This was the message that Jewish missionaries brought to the peoples of the Roman Empire.

Furthermore, the missionaries could claim to possess one of the oldest books in the world as the basis for their religion. Theirs was no human teaching, it had been revealed by the One who created and sustains the universe. And there was as much urgency for Jewish evangelists to proclaim the judgment of God on Rome as there had been for Jonah to preach judgment on Nineveh, but with, arguably, more compassion. In a culture where many were drawn to the study of philosophy, the Jewish missionaries found ready audiences wherever they went. And Jewish mission efforts were successful. Jesus said to the Jewish leaders, "You travel over land and sea to win a single convert," (Mt 23:15).

The Roman people were ready for monotheism. The Romans were getting tired of the old religion. The number of Roman gods had become large and complicated—there were almost as many deities as humans. There was a sense in the spirits of men and women that there was something higher, something beyond the selfish machinations of the present gods. It was into this environment that the Jewish evangelists brought their faith.

The Jewish God had no image and, after AD 70, no temple from which to demand sacrifice. The destruction of the temple by the Romans took away the focal point of Judaism. This actually was a benefit to the Jewish evangelists, because now their religion could also be considered a philosophy, a system for successful living—the mixture of the two creating something greater, and finer. This religion/philosophy appeared to many Romans to be superior to other religions. By following the Jewish faith not only could one pay attention to living a better life on earth, but one also could prepare for eternal life.

Another mission advantage held by Jewish missionaries was the synagogue. The synagogue developed somewhere between the fourth and third centuries BC, during the diaspora. The diaspora (*gola* in Hebrew) is the term used to describe the establishment of Jewish communities far away from Jerusalem and the temple. As Jews lived in places where there was no priesthood they needed another way to keep their faith and remember their history and culture. Jewish expatriates, unable to make use of the temple, gathered to study the Law and the prophets; if there was a competent person present, then there would be teaching or a sermon. The invention of the synagogue also provided fellowship for a people who had chosen to leave their native land.

By Jesus' time synagogues were found not only among those scattered abroad, they were also in the Jewish homeland, in Palestine and Jerusalem, alongside the rebuilt temple. And, although it may not have been their original intention, the synagogues around the world began to attract the most unlikely of attendees, gentiles! We can only imagine what a change this would have been for Jews. The word "gentiles" means "the peoples." There were the Jews—and then there were "all those others," the gentiles. The difference between Jews and gentiles, in the eyes of Jews, was greater than the difference between men and women, or slaves and masters.

But now spiritually thirsty gentiles found their way into the synagogue, attracted by the religion of one God and the moral lives of the Jewish people. The ancient Jewish historian Josephus tells us that "The Jews continued to attract a large number of Greeks to their services, making them in a sense a part of themselves."[4] If this had been followed up, the number of Jewish adherents would have significantly increased. This was not to happen, but more on this later.

The synagogues were the means for assimilating gentiles into Judaism. They attracted nonbelievers because of their close community, their strictness, and the intensity of their devotion to Yahweh and to his revealed Law. Gentiles could become complete adherents of Judaism, be circumcised, and observe the laws of Moses or merely worship in the synagogue as people who believed in the one God and the moral way of life of the Jews. The former were called "proselytes" and the later "God-fearers."

But the synagogues also served another important mission. These distant communities also provided an infrastructure that helped the Jewish leadership remain in contact with those who were not close to Jerusalem. And for that purpose a system of messengers was employed called the *shelichim*. The term comes from the Hebrew word for "send." The essential responsibility of a *shaliach* (singular) was to actively represent another. But, the *shaliach* had a specific mission to carry out; their authority extended only for that mission and it ended when the mission had been completed.

The Jewish *shelichim* were the template for the Christian apostles.

Chapter 2
Jewish Apostles

The *shelichim* were representatives of an ancient custom, which some scholars trace back to the fifth century BC. The rabbis taught that "The messenger of a man is as the man himself." The custom also had legal connotations. In fact, the *shelichim* enjoyed extraordinary legal privileges—today we would say they carried a "power of attorney," the authority to legally and morally represent another.

In the Greek translation of the Hebrew Old Testament (which, by the way, is the oldest text of the Old Testament in existence) the Hebrew word *shalach* (to send) is translated by the Greek word *apostello*! The emphasis is on someone sent with a commission—one who is authorized to represent another.

The Hebrew word *shaliach* is only translated "apostle" one time in the Greek Old Testament, in 1 Kings 14:6. In this text things had not been going well for King Jeroboam. He had turned his back on God and given support to foreign priests. When his son became ill, he looked around for help. He was too guilty to personally go to one of God's prophets, so he sent his wife instead. Jeroboam instructed his wife to go to Shiloh and speak with the prophet who had prophesied he would become king; the prophet had been right before, maybe he would be right again! But also, a bit cautious, the king told his wife to disguise herself.

The ruse did not work. As soon as the prophet heard her feet, as she came to his door, he said, "Come in, wife of Jeroboam, I am an evil apostle for you." He had bad news for her—the child would not live. In this case the prophet acted as God's messenger. With this same understanding the rabbis called Moses, Elijah, Elisha and Ezekiel *shelichim*, authorized messengers of God.

Most of the time the *shelichim* acted in financial matters. Usually they went in pairs, so that there would be no challenge to their collection. They were to procure contributions from Jewish communities far away from Jerusalem for support of the temple. A fund was raised locally by the synagogues and then received by the *shelichim* sent out by the patriarch.

When the *shelichim* went on a mission, they were actually considered to be the person or group who sent them. When they represented the chief rab-

9

bis in Jerusalem, they had the power to supervise the teaching of officers of the local Jewish communities. With their commissioning also came the power to replace leaders who were not in accord with official teaching or practice.

One of the responsibilities of the *shelichim* was to teach, usually by means of sermons in the synagogue. And, although not all scholars agree on this, Hermann Vogelstein believes they were able to appoint others who had the same authority.[5] In other words, the *shaliach* of a *shaliach* could be as the man himself!

The *shelichim* became known to the Greeks as Jewish *apostles*. Justin Martyr in his book *Dialogue With Trypho* says that anti-Christian propaganda was carried from Jerusalem by means of agents whom he describes as "picked men," "ordained" and "sent out all over the civilized world." Later the early Christian historian Eusebius, commenting on Isaiah 18:1, calls these messengers "apostles."

Another Christian writer, Epiphanius, describes the work of a Jewish apostle in the fourth century AD. Epiphanius, himself a strict constructionist on Christian doctrine, says that a certain "Joseph," was dispatched with letters from Jerusalem to the Jews of Cilicia. When he arrived he levied tithes and firstfruits from Jews throughout the province. But all did not go well. In Epiphanius' words,

> When therefore in virtue of his apostleship (for so is this order of men entitled by the Jews, as I have said) he acted with great rigor, forsooth, in his reforms and restoration of good order—which was the very business before him—deposing and removing from office many wicked chiefs of the synagogue—and priests and presbyters and ministers ... he became hated by many people.[6]

But these messengers did more than collect money and supervise teaching. The Hebrew apostles were at times representatives of the Jewish court. In this role they served documents, collected money for the court, and conveyed instructions to others. And delegates of the court called *shelichim*, prepared the high priest for the services of the Day of Atonement.

There were also *shelichim* within the synagogue communities. The *shaliach* (apostle) of the Jewish congregation officially represented the worshipping community to God. The same rule applied: the *shaliach* is as the people themselves. The rabbis taught that

> If a man in saying his private prayers makes an error in reciting the Psalms, it is a bad sign for him. But if he is saying these prayers as the "shaliach" of the congregation, it is a bad omen for the ones who appointed him.[7]

In effect, these Jewish apostles had even more clout than someone with our "power of attorney." The apostle could marry on behalf of the one who had sent them, or divorce on their behalf.

The apostle of a man could purchase and sacrifice the Passover lamb, if they had been authorized, even if that apostle were a slave.

Furthermore, the honor due to the lord was to be paid to the authorized messenger. Shameful treatment of an apostle was not so much directed against the apostle as against the lord and could not be ignored. The apostle of a person is as the person himself. But the tradition also says it is worthy for apostles to die in the performance of their duties.

The *shaliach* is a progenitor of the New Testament apostle. Jesus thus did not invent the word *apostle,* he assumed it. There was already in God's plan a well known system within which Jewish apostles were operating, a system Jesus accepted and used. Even though the two were not equivalent, Jewish and Christian apostles were much alike.

For one thing, the phrase in Mark 3:14, "He appointed ... apostles" is the literal translation of the Hebrew expression "to appoint an authorized representative" and was a part of the wording for the official induction of a Jewish apostle.

Learned members of the narrow circle of associates of the Jewish Patriarch were constantly being commissioned as apostles. In the same way the Christian apostles received their call from the circle of the disciples, the narrower circle of Jesus' associates.

Just as the Jewish apostles, the Christian apostles were sent out two by two (Mk 6:7). The "seventy" were sent out two by two (Lk 10:1). In Matthew 11:2, there are two messengers who come from John the Baptist. And in 2 Corinthians 8:19 Paul makes sure that there are two messengers who go to collect the monetary gift from the Corinthians for the needy in Jerusalem. As was the custom among the Jewish apostles, the idea was to make sure no one would be suspicious of how these funds are being handled.

On missionary journeys Paul went with Barnabas, or Paul went with Timothy or Paul went with Silas, or Titus, and Barnabas went with Mark, two by two. Timothy and Silas were a team, as were Timothy and Erastus, and Judas and Silas. Just as in the Jewish tradition, two apostles travelled together, particularly but not only when there was money involved. But there is more.

When the apostles appointed by Jesus returned from their mission, they did the thing the apostle was expected to do: they made an explicit report to the Sender (Mk 6:30, Lk 9:10).

Even before his Damascus eye-opening experience Paul was an apostle. Not an apostle of Jesus, but an apostle of the Jewish authorities. He was commissioned to go to Damascus (Acts 9:1-2), given letters of accreditation, in the same manner as a *shaliach.* He went with the power of the central authorities, to capture any Christians he might find and drag them back to Jerusalem. His intention was to bring back not simply a statement but a visible demonstration of his success: prisoners. Fortunately the tables were turned and Paul ended up the captive!

When this link between the Hebrew and Christian apostles is taken into account it gives us a deeper understanding of certain passages of Scripture. For instance, John 13:16. In this text, a fairly familiar one, Jesus has just washed the feet of The Twelve to impress on their consciences the importance of servanthood. He explained this in part by saying (via the usual English translation) "nor is he who is sent greater than he who sends him." The word in the Greek is, you guessed it, *apostle.* It added something to Jewish ears to hear Jesus say to these Twelve that the *apostle* is not above the one who sent him.

Philippians 2:25 is another example of how a knowledge of the Jewish apostle can deepen the meaning of a text. In English translations Epaphroditus (whose name in Greek means "charming" or "comely") is called a messenger. But again, the Greek says he was an *apostolos* of the Philippians.

Epaphroditus had brought money for Paul, who was in prison at the time. As a result of his exertions he became very ill. In Philippians 2:30 Paul says Epaphroditus had put his life at risk (literally, "gambled with his life") to give his support. This sounds as if he were no mere messenger. It sounds as if Epaphroditus was an apostle commissioned by the Philippian congregation to serve Paul.

Again, in 2 Corinthians 8. Even though the English translations say "messengers," the most natural translation for verse 23 would be "As for our brothers, they are *apostles* of the churches, the glory of Christ." Who were these apostles?

These men had been appointed by the churches to collect money. Those to whom they were sent were people who were used to representatives called apostles coming from Jerusalem to collect money for the temple. If we were more familiar with Judaism at the time of Jesus we would understand that in this case apostle is a better translation than messenger.

The apostles sent from the authorities in Jerusalem were typically ordained rabbis. They had been set apart for their work by the laying on of hands. And in Acts 13 Paul and Barnabus were set apart by the Antioch community, by the laying on of hands. As a result, they left Antioch to go to Cyprus. In Cyprus they preached the Word of God in the synagogues of the capital, Salamis. They were, in effect, apostles—missionaries.

This became more and more typical in the Christian community, so that later on, in the second century, Christian people understood the term "apostle" to refer to wandering missionary preachers.

But with all of the similarity between Jewish and Christian apostles there is one glaring difference: the Jewish apostle was never a missionary. The *shaliach's* work did not go beyond the Jewish community.

There were Jewish missionaries, but there were not Jewish missionaries who were ever called *shelichim* or *apostles.* The New Testament apostle goes beyond the Jewish understanding, although it contains enough elements of the Jewish apostolate to make us appreciate it's derivation. But it is not the same; the New Testament apostle has expanded beyond the original concept.

Jesus commissioned his representatives to represent him to the ends of the earth, to Jews, but also to gentiles. To believers and unbelievers.

Most important for our understanding of the phrase *apostolic church* in the Nicene Creed is to understand the role of the apostle in Judaism.

The important elements carried over from the Jewish institution are:

1. The apostle is one who is commissioned. A person could not simply choose to become someone else's apostle.
2. The commissioning brought with it the authority to represent the other, to be the other person in another place. All of the authority held by the sender is carried by the one sent.
3. This authorization is for a specific purpose. There is a task to be accomplished and the authority of the apostle is extended only for this task.

When we say the church is *apostolic* this is what we mean! The church itself is God's authorized messenger, sent with God's authority for his specific purpose: to evangelize the world.

Part II
"Then to all the apostles"
−1 Corinthians 15:7

Twelve there were who served, it's true,
    Matthew, Andrew and Bartholemew,
James the Elder, James the Less,
    John and Jude. called Thaddeus.
Simon Peter, Andrew's brother,
    Simon Zealotes was the other.
Philip brought Jesus fish and bread,
    Judas the one who wanted him dead,
But to Thomas' surprise we now are led!
    −Robert J. Scudieri[8]

By the end of the first century the Christian movement had, under God's blessings, experienced rapid growth. Christian communities were planted in Galatia, Asia, Bithynia, Pontus and Cappodocia.[9] Even though much of the church's growth, from the human point of view, was unplanned, from the divine perspective God even allowed persecution in order to spread the church. Generally it is the apostles who are given the credit. The Twelve, chosen by Jesus, were sent out for service in the kingdom of God, with full authority from God. As in the case of the rabbinic shelichim they were commissioned and authorized representatives of the One who had sent them for a specific purpose: to bring the Good News of salvation to all through faith in Jesus Christ. However, there was more.

15

Chapter 3
The Wider New Testament Use of Apostle

The Twelve apostles played a central role in the earliest church. The accepted tradition is reflected by Carl Braaten in his book *The Apostolic Imperative*. Braaten describes the New Testament apostle as:

> unique, once-for-all, and unrepeatable in later generations. After the first generation there could be no successors to the apostles .... Just as there would never have to be another Messiah, another incarnation of the Son of God, another crucifixion for the salvation of the world, another resurrection of the crucified Christ, so also there would never have to be another set of apostles, another set of primary witnesses to the risen Lord ...[10]

Apostle was the title given first to The Twelve closest disciples of Jesus, plus Matthias, Judas' replacement (Acts 1:26). In Luke and Acts they make up what appears to be a ruling body in Jerusalem (Acts 8:1), with first Peter and then James, the brother of Jesus, as their leader (Acts 15:13-19).

In Matthew 10 Jesus had sent out The Twelve as his apostles to the twelve tribes of Israel. They were to herald the news that the kingdom of Heaven was at hand. The kingdom might even come before they had preached to all the twelve tribes (Mt 10:23).

After Jesus' resurrection The Twelve apostles were authorized for an infinitely broader work: they are to go to all nations, bearing the news that the Son of God had come alive from the dead, to free all people from the power of death. They were to make disciples not only of Israelites, but of all people.

In speaking of the future and the final fulfillment of all things, our Lord frequently used concrete illustrations figuratively. So when Jesus stated that these Twelve would someday sit on twelve thrones to judge the tribes of Israel (Mt 19:28; Lk 22:30), he envisioned not only the certainty that the Gospel through them would triumph here in time, but that his church would be victoriously complete in eternity—as the perfect "New Jerusalem" with its symbolic twelve foundations and the city gates. This is beautifully pictured in Revelation 21:12 and 14.

Besides proclaiming the Good News as witnesses to the risen Christ, already here in time they were "sitting on thrones," as it were, to uphold and defend all that Christ had taught and commanded (Mt 28:20, Acts 15).

The Twelve also were administrators of the finances. Early in the history of the church the powerful love of Christ permeated the lives of individual Christians. So overwhelming was this force that Christians sold personal property, houses and land, in order to contribute to a common fund of the church to help the poor among them.

One man from Cyprus, named Joseph, sold a field he owned. Luke says Joseph brought the proceeds from the sale "and put it at the apostles' feet" (Acts 4:35). This Joseph was so well thought of that the leaders gave him a new name, Barnabas, which in Hebrew means "son of encouragement."

After a while this work of distributing funds took up so much of their time and good will that the apostles had to ask for help from the rest of the disciples. In Acts 6 this becomes the occasion for the selection of seven deacons.

But there were apostles in the early church other than the original Twelve, Matthias and Paul. Paul himself alludes to this. In 1 Corinthians 15:8 Paul calls himself an apostle and he lists all those to whom Jesus appeared after his resurrection from the dead. In the list (1 Cor 15:5-7) Paul includes Peter, The Twelve, more than five hundred brothers, James and then "all the apostles." Who were they?

Paul doesn't explain. But elsewhere Scripture does name other apostles. In Acts 14:14 Barnabas, the Son of Encouragement, is identified as an apostle together with Paul. When Paul wrote his first letter to the Christians in Thessalonica he considered at least Silvanus and probably Timothy as apostles with himself (1 Thess 2:6).

When he closed his letter to the Romans Paul asked to be remembered to Andronicus and Junia, two relatives who had been in prison with him who were outstanding "among the apostles" (Rom 16:7). The Greek text makes it clearer than the English translation that Paul considers them apostles.

As T. W. Manson, the eminent New Testament scholar wrote in *The Church's Ministry,* "It seems clear that we have to reckon with a stricter and a looser use of the term both in the New Testament and in early Christian literature."[11]

Many of the Christian writers immediately following the New Testament period used the term apostle broadly and inconsistently. There seemed to be no rigid limitation to the office.[12] At the end of the first century, the writing titled *The Teaching of the Twelve Apostles,* better known as the *Didache,* assumed only a broader use of the title apostle! Interesting, since the title itself would seem to narrow the designation.

In *1 Clement, The Letter of the Romans to the Corinthians,* written before AD 100, Apollos is called an apostle (47:4).

In later Christian writings the same can be seen. Origen (d. 254) calls the Samaritan woman of John 4 an apostle, because she brought the Gospel to her neighbors.[13] Eusebius of Caeserea (d. 339) says that "many apostles remained in Jerusalem until its fall." Could this have been "many of the Twelve"? Or, was Eusebius referring to the broader designation, "missionaries" who were being sent out into all the world?

Gregory of Antioch described the women at Jesus' grave as apostles because they had been sent by God; Stephen is called an apostle by Didymus Alexandrinus; Gregory Nazianzus considers Mark an apostle.

Early on the broader and narrower meanings of *apostle* were used side by side, until the narrow interpretation won out. Ignatius, writing in the early second century, only used the narrow definition.

There are even some who (on the basis of Galatians 2:7) suggest that there were only two apostles, Peter for the Jews (1 Pet 1:1) and Paul for the gentiles (1 Tim 2:7)!

The early church apologist Tertullian argued for a much larger number. He suggested that there were eighty-two apostles, counting along with The Twelve the seventy whom Jesus had "sent" out (Lk 10:1). And for proof he pointed to the Old Testament, specifically, to Exodus 15:27, where the itinerant Israelites stopped at Elim. According to Tertullian, there were certainly twelve wells of water, but they were accompanied by "three score and ten palm trees"!

In fact even if the seventy are nowhere called apostles in the New Testament, the Greek word for "sent out" in Luke 10:1 is *apostellein*. And, in reference to the mission of The Twelve, they, the additional persons, are spoken of as "seventy others" (some manuscripts say "seventy-two").

There is ample evidence to believe that the designation apostle was held by others. Undoubtedly they stood in the shadow of The Twelve, but in function, as sent ones, they remain visible in the church right up to today.

How can this be explained?

First, we must look at the rabbinic institution of the *shelichim*. In Matthew 10:1 the Gospel writer began his account of the mission of The Twelve by calling them the *disciples*. In verse two they are called *apostles*. What has happened in between to change things? A *commissioning*, by Jesus, authorizing his representatives to carry on a specific task, to announce the arrival of the kingdom (cf. Mk 3:14, Lk 6:13).

Paul also emphasized his equality with the other apostles by pointing to his commissioning by Christ as a *shaliach*. He makes it a point in Galatians 1:1 that his apostleship came from Jesus and God the Father. He is a personal representative of God, a *shaliach* of God.

In the New Testament the word *apostellein* is used when the technical sense of authorizing someone for a task is intended. The other word for send, *pempein,* is used when it is a matter of sending someone on an ordinary mission.[14] However, apostles (in the broader sense) continue to represent Christian communities, just as the *shelichim* would represent Jewish communities.

As the Jews used apostles for official business, so did the followers of Jesus. Epaphroditus had been commissioned by the Philippians (Phil 2:25). The "representatives of the churches" in 2 Corinthians 8:23 became involved in the collection of funds for Jerusalem. In addition, they were "successor apostles," that is, sent ones who followed in the train of The Twelve.

Christian apostles exercised supervision, as did the Jewish apostles. In Acts 8:14 Peter and John, among the original Twelve, were sent out by the apostles in Jerusalem to look into Philip's new mission in Samaria. They found the work incomplete and took steps to regularize it, that is, "that they might receive the Holy Spirit."

While in Samaria they met a sorcerer by the name of Simon who had attached himself to Philip. Apparently Simon had not learned much Christian doctrine, because when he saw the Holy Spirit come upon the Samaritans he offered Peter and John a bribe so that he could have the same power. He misunderstood from where their apostleship had come. Peter and John were offended that he would demean their commission by offering them money.

At this time mission work was expanding rapidly even without authorized planters. It was difficult to control the preaching and teaching of the faith. The field in Antioch grew beyond anything that was dreamed. And so there developed the troubling issue of whether converts had to be circumcised. At the Jerusalem Council (Acts 15) the decision was reached not to require this observance of Old Testament law. The council then commissioned Judas and Silas and gave them letters (just as was the custom among the Jewish apostles) to go to Antioch with Paul and Barnabus, to announce the decision.

In Acts 16 Paul and Timothy are described as going from village to village, delivering the consensus reached by the leaders in Jerusalem. The Holy Spirit guided them. They were apostles of God, going where God led them. And God's guidance sometimes changed their course. They were kept out of Asia. When they tried to enter Bithynia they were turned away. The Lord's will became clear to them when they reach Troas; there a vision in the night instructed Paul to go over to Macedonia, and so enter Europe.

The Christians of the first century as they began to organize looked first to their own heritage of Jewish institutions. One of those was the *shelichim,* apostles, that is, authorized messengers who represented a group or a person. As such they actually carried the authority of that group or person as they went about their assignment.

But this was not the only influence on the church's use of apostleship. There was another group that was active at the time which very well may have influenced the strategy of the Christian leadership.

As has already been pointed out, as similar as the Jewish apostles are to the Christian apostles there is one major difference—the early Jewish *she-lichim* were never missionaries. There was, however, a group active during Paul's time which utilized missionaries, and called them *apostles.* They were the Gnostics.[15]

Gnosticism was a religion that preached a "gospel" of redemption from the physical world. To Gnostics the physical world was evil. Salvation could happen only if a person's soul were freed from the body. This occurred when the individual learned secret knowledge, known only to the Gnostics. It was the burden of the Gnostic "apostles" to communicate that knowledge. And in the course of their work they did cross paths with missionaries of the early Christian church.

Antioch in Syria became one of the early strongholds of gentile Christianity. Luke tells us that the Christians who were scattered by persecutions in Jerusalem that followed the stoning of Stephen, told the message of Jesus only to Jews as far as Phonecia, Cyprus and Antioch. But some men from Cyprus and Cyrene "went to Antioch and began to speak to Greeks also, telling them the Good News about the Lord Jesus" (Acts 11:19-20).

Thus Antioch, the third largest city in the Roman empire, became the gentile center of the church from which Paul's three missionary journeys were launched.

It was in Antioch that the followers of Jesus were first called "Christians" (Acts 11:26). It is plausible that Antioch was the place where the term *apostle* was first used in a broader sense to refer to messengers of the churches.

Gnostic missionaries had penetrated this busy center of travel and trade, rubbing elbows with Christians. Gnostics existed prior to the time of Jesus' earthly pilgrimage, but in Jesus' teaching they saw a similarity to their own beliefs. At first the Gnostics may have shown an interest in this new Jewish Christian movement, and so the Christians would not have immediately resisted.

It was not long before Gnosticism had incorporated the Lord into its world view. Jesus became the One who had descended to earth to reveal the secret knowledge necessary for eternal life. Eventually the contacts between Christians and Gnostics went beyond disagreements and became acrimonious. Gnostics claimed that they alone knew Jesus' secrets; he had informed only them of the truths that could liberate people from their bodies. If at first certain Christians saw a potential for leading Gnostics to Christ, they ultimately saw in Gnosticism only heresy.

The missionary of Gnosticism was called a *delegate,* a sent one (i.e., an apostle in the broader sense). He possessed the divine knowledge (the mysteries) which could bring salvation. The Gnostic apostles saw themselves as on the same level as everyone else in the community, not superior, and were always concerned to assist their hearers to find the same self understanding which they had attained. In that sense they were missionary oriented.

They even went on mission tours. "In Galatia, Philippi and Corinth they do mission work in the tracks of Paul."[16] This began to put young Christian congregations in jeopardy. These Gnostic "apostles" may very well have been the "false apostles" and "super-apostles" Paul attacked in 2 Corinthians 11. These anti-Christian missionaries taught salvation by good works, brushing aside the Good News of salvation by grace alone through faith in Jesus.

Rabbinic and Gnostic apostles affected the early church's view of the Christian apostle, yet there is one final influence on the Christian understanding of apostle that outweighs both the rabbinic and Gnostic understanding.

The example of the early apostles is not the only or major source for the term apostolic church. The key for understanding the term *apostolic church* comes from the first and ultimate Apostle of God.

Jesus is God's Apostle (Heb 3:1). Think what that means: commissioned by God he comes with the authority of God. The office of an apostle means not just that the sender and the one sent are *somehow* linked; no—the understanding is that the sender and the one sent are *united*. Jesus as God's Son is God on earth. In Luke 5:23 he does what no other human being could claim to do, he forgives sin.

Previous to this God had sent others. Abraham, Moses, Elijah, the prophets. But then, at the right time, God chose to *send* his Son (Gal 4:4). The Son is the greatest revelation (Heb 1:1-3). In John 17:18 and John 20:21 Jesus proclaimed that he was commissioned and authorized by God his Father. By this authorization he also sent others.

So Jesus came first. He is the Model for the apostleship of all others. The first Apostles and the apostolic church should not be surprised if they are not always accepted, loved and supported. The pattern is laid down in Matthew 21:37 in the parable of the householder who authorized his son to go and check on some holdings. Those who were to be watching over these holdings (vineyards) watched over them jealously and begrudged the owner what was his. In contempt for the owner they killed the son. The reference is clearly to the ministry of Jesus and just as clearly to the messengers of his church whom he sends.

The apostles sent out by Jesus did not even speak on their own. They are not the subject of their message. In Matthew 10:18-20 Jesus instructed them that when they are dragged before secular authorities and give their witness, "It is not you who speak, but the Spirit of your Father speaking through you."

Jesus is the Archetype for the apostolic church, as he was for the first Apostles. The Apostles had to drink that same cup Jesus drank in Gethsemane and on Golgotha. As Christianity became distinctively different from the cultural cloak of Judaism it became more and more conspicuous, and less and less tolerated.

Emperor Nero, needing a scapegoat for the terrible fire in Rome in AD 64 (which many believed he had set), chose to accuse Christians, whom he believed were members of "an extremely pernicious superstition."[17] According to J. B. Lightfoot, for the Roman, religion was really a matter for the government. The primary function of religion was to protect the interests of the empire. Refusing to acknowledge the emperor as God or to offer a sacrifice to him was therefore "pernicious." Christians were persecuted as guilty of treason and therefore they deserved to die.

But Christians were willing to accept pain, even death, because Jesus had accepted it, and because they knew this age was not going to last very long.

The apostle was willing therefore to be hungry and thirsty (1 Cor 4:11-12), to suffer incessantly, although without despair (2 Cor 4:7-18; Phil 3:8-11). Apostles were arrested and put into prison (Acts 5:18). They were whipped, ordered not to preach any more in the Name of Jesus (Acts 5:40) but they went right back out and did just that (Acts 5:41-42).

Indeed, for the apostle, suffering was something "divinely willed" and he "boasted" of it (2 Cor 11:16, 12:10, Gal 6:17, 1 Thess 3:3). They were sad spectacles to the world, to human beings and even angels (1 Cor 4:9). In short, they were Christ-like as they performed their mission as his sent ones. Though weak, in him they could endure all things.

Chapter 4
New Testament Apostles Were Missionaries

The Latin word for send is *mittere* and the Greek word is *apostellein*. First and foremost, the early Christian apostles acted, spoke, thought and taught as "sent ones," as missionaries. And this is how they were understood by those who knew them and later by many who wrote about them.

The middle and later part of the first century were times ripe for Christian mission efforts. Almost everywhere in the Roman Empire citizens knew the Greek language; further, the Roman Empire had brought a political unity to the nations bordering the Mediterranean. This linguistic and political unity guaranteed the growth and security of international traffic over an admirable system of Roman roads.

Travel throughout the empire also led to a mixed population in the large cities with no common cultural heritage to bind them together. Roman law, however also helped to unify the empire and promoted human rights, even for minorities. During the first century ancient society was beginning to decompose. Change was in the wind. People were restless for something that would catch their imagination and hold their hearts.

Consequently at this time there was a new fondness for philosophy, especially for any which contained elements of mystery. There was also a desire for revelation and miracles. Most importantly, Rome's policy of religious tolerance provided a climate of freedom for beliefs, at least as long as they did not conflict with the state religion.

The time was right for mission work. There was serious discussion concerning many matters in the early church, yes, even spectacular disagreements. Even so, the people knew their mission. For early Christianity mission meant winning and enlisting converts.

Apostles were missionaries who planted churches; they were individuals who witnessed to the resurrection of Christ and called many to faith in him. At the end of the first century, if the phrase *apostolic church* had been used (and there is no evidence that it was), it would have meant *missionary church*, the church of the "sent ones."

An insight of Eusebius demonstrates this. This "father of church history," as he is sometimes known, became the bishop of Caesarea in AD 313.

Among other works he wrote a chronology of the church, an account of martyrdoms in Palestine between AD 303 and 310, and a biography of the Emperor Constantine. But the project for which he is best known is *Historia Ecclesiastica* (*History of the Church*).

In this latter book Eusebius described how the apostles assembled in Jerusalem to divide the spheres of their missionary work. There is a tradition, recounted by Kenneth Scott Latourette, that Thomas was to evangelize the Parthians, Matthew Ethiopia, Bartholomew India and Andrew Scythia.

In church work (as in other vocations) there needs to be a readiness to follow the prompting and leading of the Holy Spirit. A classic example is that of St. Paul, who had planned to work in Bithynia, but the Spirit indicated otherwise (Acts 16:6-9). The same was true for Thomas, if the following tradition is accurate.

Thomas the Apostle is supposed to have been brought to India as the slave of a carpenter, named Abbanes. One of the kings in India, a monarch known as Gundaphorus, commanded Thomas to build him a palace. Instead, the apostle decided to build the king not a physical palace, but a spiritual home in heaven. In other words, he distributed the money he had been given for the palace to the poor.

When eventually the king demanded to see his palace, Thomas cheerfully answered, "You cannot see it now, but when you depart this life, you will see it." Allegedly the king became furious and put Thomas into jail. Later on, the story goes, the king became a Christian, was baptized, and so God's plan was accomplished.

Whether or not these traditions are history, they demonstrate how the apostles were perceived by the early church. The best evidence, however, is still the New Testament. When Paul and Barnabus were called apostles in Acts 14:14 they were in the middle of a missionary journey. Their work was met with violent opposition. In Iconius there were public demonstrations and near stoning.

In Lystra, after healing a lame man, the leaders and crowds tried to deify Paul and Barnabas. Paul was actually stoned and presumed dead (Acts 14:8-20). In this manner Paul and Barnabas were forced to move on, carrying the Gospel to other cities.

It was to the apostles that Jesus had entrusted the continuation of his mission (Jn 17:18, Lk 24:47, Mt 28:16-20). Paul's lament in 1 Corinthians 9:5 is indirect evidence that other apostles also went on missionary journeys: why isn't *he* allowed to take a wife along on his missionary travels, since the other apostles "and the Lord's brothers and Cephas" were doing just that?

The apostles of the New Testament founded churches. The following list of different categories of workers gives us, not the order of importance, but of priority:

And in the church God has appointed first of all apostles, second prophets, third teachers, then workers of miracles, also those having gifts of healing, those able to help others, those with gifts of administration, and those speaking in different kinds of tongues. (1 Cor 12:28)

In other words, Paul was giving us a chronological order in the establishment of new congregations.

It is clear that the first apostles were commissioned by Christ himself and were given his authority– "He who receives you, receives me" (Mt 10:40), "He who listens to you listens to me" (Lk 10:16; cf. 1 Cor 3:21-23). They became the extension of the ministry of Christ in reconciling the world to God.

Trying to prove that the apostles were primarily missionaries may seem too obvious, such as trying to prove the Statue of Liberty stands in New York Harbor, or the Eiffel tower in Paris. Yet if I were to say, "such as Columbus discovered America" you would stop me. And there is the problem.

Most Americans know the name Columbus, but do not know very much about him—only that he probably did not discover the America we know as the U.S.A. Many wonder why he deserves to have a holiday named after him. Similarly, the majority of Christian people know there were apostles but do not know who they were. Most could not even tell you the names of these closest associates of Jesus. They know some names, but very little about the apostles. Quite likely many do not know the derivation of the term *apostle*.

What was an apostle? The apostle was a commissioned missionary, authorized for evangelistic work in territories which did not yet know Jesus as Lord.

Their primary strategy was itinerant preaching. This was the same strategy given to The Twelve Jesus commissioned in the tenth chapter of Matthew. In verse seven they are told to "preach that the kingdom of heaven is near." In 1 Timothy 2:7 Paul claims he has been made a "herald and an apostle" and in 2 Timothy 4:2 he tells his protege to "preach the word, be prepared in season and out of season, correct, rebuke, encourage...." In the first century, outreach was via sermons in the synagogues, in homes, in the marketplace, wherever ordinary people spent time together (Acts 13:14; 14:1-2, 6-7; 17:22; 18:4).

And when they preached, the apostles did not choose their own topic—it was assigned to them, "Jesus Christ and him crucified" (1 Cor 2:2).

They preached the Gospel, perceived as foolishness by the "Greeks" and a stumbling block to the Jews. The main point of their preaching was Jesus' resurrection (2 Tim 1:1, 11). They preached that Jesus had been killed on a cross, and then God the Father brought him back to life. This became Good News—new life, eternal life had now been won for all people. In preaching this Good News they focused on the historical events of Jesus' life, particularly the things that happened between his arrest and his ascension into heaven. The apostolic message is summarized in Acts 2:22-40; Jesus, who was God, lived the life of a human being on earth. He died on a cross to take the punishment for our sins and was raised to life by the power of God the Father. All who live by faith in Jesus will live with him in eternity.

Those who were witnesses to apostolic preaching say it was given with great power (Acts 4:33). By the power of the Holy Spirit they were possessed with a commitment to mission, driven not by legalistic obedience, but by the love of Christ, which filled them with a sense of eschatological urgency. The apostles were gripped by a conviction that the world would end at any moment with the return of the Lord Jesus (his second coming). They eagerly awaited and prayed for this to happen. They had been instructed that they would suffer in their work, and that this suffering would be a part of the gospel's penetration into every part of the world.

Just two days before the Last Supper Jesus sat with four of his apostles, Peter, James, John and Andrew on the Mount of Olives, across from the beautiful temple (Mk 13:3). Jesus had some serious business to discuss with them. Among other things, he warned them about people who would try to deceive them, about wars that were to come, about sufferings from earthquakes and famines. He predicted that these four would be arrested and beaten up. The coming days would at times be so terrible God's people would be praying for the end of the world!

But before the end "This Gospel of the kingdom will be preached to the whole world" (Mt 24:14). Then Jesus would return and gather up his own from all the ends of the earth (Mk 13:27). After telling these apostles this series of events, he gave them the command to stay on their guard, to "watch" (Mk 13:37). It is in this context of our Lord's admonition to be watchful and expectant for the end that we must evaluate the apostles' sense of urgency.

We should remember that at this particular time in Jewish history there was a Jewish missionary movement. In the first century AD large numbers of gentiles had been won to Judaism because of the willingness of Jews to accommodate the faith. As a result, gentiles felt at home in many Jewish communities.[18]

Greek Judaism, which was "ardently missionary,"[19] set patterns and precedents which Christians could easily adapt in doing mission work. In fact, Jewish mission work was now at its zenith.[20] Not that there wasn't any opposition to bringing gentiles into Abraham's covenant—there certainly was. In fact the opposition eventually terminated Jewish missions.

The rabbi Shammai claimed he was not in principle an opponent of Jewish mission work, "But he subjected it to the most vigorous conditions." The eighteen rules which he laid down included, among other things, the prohibition against learning Greek, and another against accepting presents from pagans for the temple."[21] Eventually Shammai's parochial point of view prevailed. This contributed to the death of Jewish missionary work.

Jews wanted even less to save the gentiles after the defeat of the Jewish revolution in AD 70. Then very exclusivistic tendencies among Jews reasserted themselves, in part as an effort to preserve the uniqueness of the Jewish people. Sometimes self preservation is a stronger impulse than mission outreach. That has been known to be the case even today.

More and more the church of Jesus stood out from the Jewish community. The gentile Christian churches in Antioch, Syria and Cilicia did not observe the complete Jewish ceremonial law, but they continued to stay in touch with the home base in Jerusalem, and wanted her recognition (Acts 15:1-2, 23f). According to Harnack, they considered sacrifice "useless" and ceremonial law "was to be interpreted allegorically."[22]

With the fall of Jerusalem in AD 70 Christianity inherited the strongholds which had been established by the Jewish missionaries.[23] It was St. Paul, perhaps using what he had learned about the need for missions under Gamaliel, who made effective use of these former Jewish mission centers. And it was Paul, who was called and led by the Holy Spirit, who established Christianity firmly among the gentiles. But Paul was not the first to bring the Gospel to the gentiles.

In Acts 10 Peter preached to Cornelius in the seaport of Caesarea. Through a God-given vision he also received a lesson in what was important and what was not. What food goes into a person was not important, at least not for their spirituality. As a result not only Cornelius and his family were converted, but Peter was converted to the idea that reaching the gentiles with the Gospel was important in God's scheme of things.

Without denigrating Paul's special place "as a chosen vessel of God," it can be said that Paul wasn't even second, or third to reach non-Jews with the Gospel. Luke says some anonymous "natives of Cypress and Cyrene" (Acts 11:20), escaping from the persecution of Christians that broke out after Stephen was murdered, began to work in Antioch among gentiles.

After a while the gentile Christian mission centers took over the mission initiative, stamping the Christian mission into its final mold—and Antioch was the leader.

Overlooking the navigable Orontes river, Antioch was an excellent seaport city. It was also the capital of the Roman province of Syria and the third largest city in the Roman Empire. In effect, Antioch became for gentile Christians what Jerusalem was for Jewish Christians: an epicenter of mission work. From Antioch the Christian Gospel reverberated among gentiles even hundreds of miles away. The shock waves would be felt for centuries. But most immediately they shook a rabbi from Tarsus.

Saul of Tarsus (Acts 9; Gal 1:13-2:10) became a Christian missionary in Antioch. He already had become a Christian and spent several years studying the new faith. He learned the ropes from Barnabas, the one who had donated one of his properties for Christian charity work. Barnabas had been commissioned by the leadership in Jerusalem to supervise this extraordinary mission opportunity in Antioch. When Barnabas arrived in Antioch he found there was too much work for one person, and so he took the time to find Paul and bring him back as an assistant (Acts 11:22-26). The assistant later became the director.

By the end of Paul's life (about AD 66) and Nero's rule (AD 68) Christianity had spread throughout a good deal of the eastern Mediterranean area. The church in Antioch was a leader in planting new churches—teams commissioned in Antioch (including Paul and Barnabas) had established young congregations throughout Galatia, western Asia Minor and several important cities in Greece, including Philippi, Thessalonica and Corinth.[24] It wasn't Jerusalem that was the center for early Christian mission work among gentiles, but Antioch.

Luke, a Greek-speaking Christian (possibly from Antioch) uses the word apostle much more than any other writer, more even than Paul. Would it be too far fetched to imagine that Greek missionaries from Antioch, such as Paul, trying to find an official title to signify they had been authorized to carry out their work were the first to settle on the word *apostle*? Of course Jesus called The Twelve he had commissioned *apostles* (Lk 6:13); now, however, the term is broadened to refer in a wider sense to Christian missionaries.

It is entirely possible that as the name Christian was coined in Antioch, the term *apostle* used in a wider sense for Christian missionaries also could have originated here.

The apostles, in the broad sense, were missionaries. What does that say for an *apostolic church*? It says that the church is "established on the foundation of the apostles and prophets" insofar as it too is missionary. But only because Jesus was *missionary,* sent, since he is the "chief cornerstone" (Eph 2:20). He was sent by his Father, for the specific purpose of finding the lost (Lk 19:10).

The church is apostolic not just because it represents the apostles' teaching, but because it re-presents Christ.

As the church expanded to cover the whole known world, the office of the apostle died out! Why? Was there more to it than the death of The Twelve who were divinely appointed by Jesus as eyewitnesses? What did it mean for the *church* to be apostolic in the second, third and early fourth centuries?

Part III
"Welcomed as if he were the Lord."
–The Didache 11.4

How was mission work carried out after the death of the apostles? The work did not end with their demise; the church remained apostolic even after the apostles were gone. One thing I discovered about the next generation of Christian mission work was that it was not a plan that brought Christianity to all parts of the known world—at least not a human plan.

To understand how the church was apostolic in the second and third centuries we need to first survey the place of the church in the Roman Empire, then ask how mission work was carried out. This will put us in a position to understand the meaning of the phrase *apostolic church*.

Chapter 5
The Early Church In the Roman Empire

The church grew in a world controlled by one government with an empire wide common language. Early growth in the church was rapid and effective. According to Luke, on the morning of Pentecost there were "about one hundred and twenty persons" gathered together (Acts 1:15), a tenfold increase from the Twelve. By the end of the day there were "about three thousand" disciples, people who "accepted the message and were baptized" (Acts 2:41). The joy quickly spread. Soon the numbers swelled to five thousand (Acts 4:4) and by Acts 21:20, there were uncounted "thousands of Jews" who were brought to faith. Luke indicates these people were not just hangers-on, but individuals who believed and were "zealous for the law."

The churches were concentrated in the larger cities but were also visible in towns of all sizes. The majority of Christians were from the poorer free levels of society—with little attention paid to evangelization of slaves.[25]

In the beginning the growth of the church was within the Jewish community—but this did not last for long. External conditions assured continued expansion among Jews, but even more so among gentiles. At this time there was a movement towards monotheism and "a common yearning for salvation."[26] The spirituality of people in the Roman Empire was undernourished, with serious disrupting effects. The empire had been bound together in part by a devotion to the emperor and to common gods; it was to these gods that the leadership credited military, economic and social success.

For a long time, before Jesus entered Jerusalem, the state and family religious cults were losing their influence. More and more they were unable to satisfy some of the needs for which a large growing proportion of the empire looked to religion. Even the leaders of the state's religion were suspect. "Ceremonies were maintained as a matter of public policy, but no test was applied to insure the endorsement of the existence of gods by those officiating."[27]

In the first two centuries after Jesus, philosophy became increasingly popular. Numerous peripatetic philosophers, such as Paul encountered in Athens, toured the world trying to do what the official religion was not able to do: to raise the morality of the people. Lecture halls became common in the cities of the Roman Empire.[28] There was a thirst also for spiritual knowledge (cf. Paul at Ephesus in Acts 19).

In the second and third centuries the church began to react to the culture. Increasing numbers of Christians made this inevitable. The reaction brought significant change to the church. Even though individual Christian communities remained small, by AD 180 there were churches in all the provinces of the empire and in Mesopotamia.[29] But all over the world Christians understood themselves to be on a temporary journey on earth. Heaven was their real home, and Jesus was going to return in the immediate future to take them there.

At the beginning of the third century there were fairly clear restrictions on Christian involvement in matters of this earth, a place where they were going to continue only for a while.

Certain professions were off limits—such as teaching children "worldly knowledge," acting, producing shows, joining the military, becoming a civil magistrate. The last four were put on the same level as earning a living as an astrologer or a prostitute.[30] Christians had not been allowed to become involved in the business of this world—it might have taken their minds off the imminence of the next. Now that began to change.

Even at the beginning of the second century there were signs of more involvement with the world. There are examples in this period of popular stories from the secular world retold with a Christian twist. In the apocryphal *Acts of Paul* there is a Christianized version of the story of Androcles and the lion. Because of laws enacted by the empire to curtail religions that might pose a threat to the state religion, churches were not allowed to own property. Initially this was not a problem; small groups of Christians met in homes of members. But as more and more became followers of Christ, larger spaces were required.

In the third century, while Christians continued to meet in homes, some took over entire houses, large houses. Houses were remodeled for use as church buildings. Three rooms were essential: a large assembly room, a back room for adult instruction and private confession, and a dining room was needed for the fellowship meals. There was also a need for storage space and living quarters.[31]

This growth can actually be charted at Dura-Europos, east of the Euphrates. The Christians started a church in a house of reasonable size built around a courtyard.[32] As the church grew, renovations were made: they started meeting in a small room off of the courtyard. Later, some time around AD 240, a larger hall was built with room for eighty people by knocking out a wall and making two rooms into one. On the door to the street was a red cross, signifying that it was a "church house," private but with public uses.[33]

The church was developing into a strong influence on the Roman empire, growing in authority and temporal power. At times that power was abused.

The challenge of ownership was sometimes met by having one of the deacons own the property. This was bound to cause problems, and Origen, one of the early church leaders, tells us that there were cases where deacons "confused" church and personal funds.

In time Christians could hold and influence positions of leadership in the world, from which they were able to benefit each other. As an example there is a story about a bishop in Syria who convinced many Christians of the impending judgement and that they should go out into the desert to meet Christ. Without responsible leadership or organization, those Christians wandered aimlessly in the mountains. Concerned neighbors reported this to the authorities who began arresting the pilgrims under suspicion they might be planning robberies. It so happened that the wife of the governor of Syria was a Christian, so she interceded and saved those poor people from further arrest and execution as bandits.[34]

By the beginning of the third century Christian people were expecting to be on earth for a longer period of time. With this shift, more attention was paid to making plans for this life. Even the liturgy underwent changes: it became more elaborate, longer and laid "more emphasis on thanksgiving than on petition for deliverance" from this world.[35]

The church of the third century benefited from a skeletal, but strong administrative structure. Records show that the Bishop of Rome had a staff of one hundred and fifty-four, including fifty-two exorcists, forty-six presbyters, seven deacons, seven subdeacons and forty-two acolytes (that does not include readers and doorkeepers). At that time the church was ministering to "more than fifteen hundred widows and poor people" from a common fund. Besides this, the clergy were receiving a monthly salary.[36] Rome was not only the center of Christian orthodoxy in the third century, but also the center of Christian finance.

For the first two centuries the church suffered through periods of persecution, troubling times which retarded expansion. If Christianity had remained a Jewish denomination the Romans would not have bothered with it. The church could have remained protected under the leniency enjoyed by the Jews. And, it probably would not have grown to the point where it threatened the old Roman religion with mass departures from the worship of their gods, the gods Romans believed had lifted Rome to the height of power.[37] An edict on marriage in AD 295 proclaimed,

> The Roman Empire has attained its present greatness by the favor of all deities only because it has protected all its laws with wise religious observance and concern for morality.[38]

An old saying claims that "the blood of the martyrs is the seed of the church," but the seed bore more fruit once the memory of executions had died away. In AD 260, for all intents and purposes, persecution stopped. Until AD 303 there were no general arrests, imprisonments or murder of Christians. In fact, the only place where Christian people were discriminated against widely was the Roman army, which continued to celebrate the old state religion. Finally, even the right to hold church property was recognized.

Christians enjoyed the benefits of a trusting empire, until early in the fourth century. Then things turned evil. The lowest ebb is the turn of the tide, and that ebb came for Christians early in the fourth century AD, on February 23, 303.

At that time the Roman Empire was under stress. Crop failures caused famines, disease brought death. There was constant military pressure from groups outside and inside the government. A fire in the Emperor's palace in the Eastern capital at Nicomedia was blamed on Christians. Wanting to appease the old gods and avenge the destruction of his palace, the emperor set the festival of the "Terminalia" for the end of Christianity. As the sun rose imperial soldiers broke into the church nearest the palace to loot and then burn it. On the following day an edict was published which said all churches were to be destroyed, Christian assemblies were forbidden and Christian scriptures were to be burned. Any Christians of rank were to lose all their privileges and "Imperial servants who were Christians were to be reduced to slavery."[39]

There was only one other official persecution, from AD 308 to 311. However, the number of Christians who lost their lives was small. In 311 the Emperor Galerius issued an edict of toleration restoring the rights of Christians. In his edict Galerius simply declared that he had been victorious, that the Christians, after being ordered to return to the worship of the pagan gods had done so, and he was now lifting his ban. All this was not true, but the lie served the cause of peace. Christians were allowed to rebuild their churches and continued to live as they had before.

As the church regrouped it now continued to grow. Bishops and presbyters took on greater authority, so that by Constantine's time the Emperor recognized in Christianity the potential for a very influential ally.

The alliance between the Christian church and the Constantinian state reshaped the way Christian missionary work was carried out. In the end this alliance moved the church still farther away from its understanding of *apostolos* as *missionary,* and gave the term *apostolic church* the primary meaning of *official church.* That is the story we will come back to, but first we need to ask how missionary work continued after the apostles had passed away up until the time of Constantine.

Chapter 6
Mission Work in the Second and Third Centuries

As has been noted, the church had a history of continual growth from the first through the early fourth century. However, the sources of that growth, along with the methods, are weighed on different scales.

There is disagreement on whether the success of Christianity was due to the work of individual missionaries (the historian Kenneth Scott Latourette supports this view) or to its institutional character (the philosopher and historian Adolph Harnack prefers this interpretation). It would be easy to affirm both the efforts of individuals and the attractive aspects of the institution, but I prefer not to temporize and so have decided to come down on the side of the institution.

The people who penetrated the known world with Jesus' Gospel were not professionals. There were no regularly paid missionaries. But still the church grew in numbers and influence. The Christian faith was carried by individual Christians, men and women, who made their living in some secular way and who "spoke of their faith to those whom they met in a natural fashion."[40] But all of these people were connected by a new reality, something never before seen on earth. The bond of fellowship created by the Holy Spirit who blessed their Gospel witness was a strong one. This peculiar power and blessing of the Holy Spirit is the cause of the success of the Christian faith.

This can be seen in Matthew 28:18-20. The key to this passage is found in verse seventeen, where Matthew observes "They worshiped him [Jesus] but some doubted." How could they have doubted Jesus? They had been with him for some time, had seen, talked and even eaten with him! How could they now "doubt"?

The Greek word for doubt in this verse means to try to stand in two places at the same time. It is used in Matthew only one other time (14:31), when Jesus walked on the water. He had come to the disciples at night, when a strong wind was causing huge waves on Lake Galilee. At first the disciples were terrified, thinking he was a ghost (v 26). But Jesus calmed them, "It is I. Don't be afraid" (v 27). Then Peter called out, "Lord, if it is you, tell me to come to you on the water." Jesus called Peter out, "Come," and he walked on the water with Jesus!

But Matthew says (v 30) Peter "saw the wind", he was afraid and began to sink. Jesus pulled him back up, and it is then that Jesus said, "Why did you doubt?" Peter had taken his eyes off of Jesus (Mt 14:22-33).

At the end of Matthew 28 the disciples realized Jesus was about to leave them, and they are afraid. They didn't doubt Jesus, they doubted themselves, their ability to carry on after Jesus left. In response to their fear Jesus promised that since all authority in heaven and on earth had been given to him they were to go out and make disciples on his behalf, by baptizing and teaching. But he would always be with them, right up to the time he would come again as victorious king of all the earth.

This same point is made in John's Gospel immediately after Judas left the last supper (Jn 13:27ff). A troubled Jesus tried to make the disciples understand that he was not going to be with them much longer. Frightened by this revelation the disciples protested, "Lord, where are you going?" (Jn 13:36). Jesus' explanation fell on their clouded understanding.

So in the fourteenth chapter of John, the Savior says in verse 18, "I will not leave you as orphans; I will come to you." This is the new factor. This is the new dimension. Jesus sent them but the Holy Spirit would be with the disciples to guide them. The ministry of Jesus was now set free from the physical body of Jesus, set free from the limits imposed by space and barriers—even the disappointment, fear and falseness of human beings.

The body of Christ is now at work through the believing community. The end of apostolic work was a local congregation "and the local congregation, as part of the Body of Christ, itself enters into the apostolic ministry."[41]

Christianity spread normally although not exclusively through the planting of churches. These churches were missionary communities. Right from the beginning the spontaneous outreach of the whole Christian community gave great impetus to the spread of Jesus' Gospel. The purpose of the congregations was to evangelize and incorporate new people into the body of Christ.

At first the efforts of new congregations were focused locally. However, it was not long before these communities radiant with faith would reach out beyond their own locale to distant areas where the faith needed to take root. As already noted, during the lifetime of the Apostles, by AD 65, there were core congregations in all parts of the Mediterranean world. How was this possible? What was it that caused the first congregations of Christians to become so focused on mission?

The earliest churches knew they were "the covenant people of God who were charged with the task of converting 'all the nations'."[42]

Because they were ignited by the surprise of Easter and fueled by the fires of Pentecost, they were possessed by a burning desire to proclaim the

Good News far and wide. In the most creative moment since the dawn of the first sun, God's Son had died and had burst back into life.

So in many cases the first action of a new Christian after baptism was to sell their belongings (Acts 4:32-37), and gave the money to the church to distribute. Some left their homes to become mendicants, beggars who knew where the bread was, trying to share that knowledge for the salvation of others. They were happy simply to bring the Gospel to where it had not yet been rooted and then appointed others to the responsibility for building up the church. And this was not only typical of the church in the first century.

In the third century Origen, one of the church fathers, gives evidence of Christians with a similar burning conviction. In AD 248 he replied to the anti-Christian teacher Celsus,

> Christians do all in their power to spread the faith all over the world. Some of them accordingly make it the business of their lives to wander not only from city to city but from town to town and village to village in order to win fresh converts for the Lord.... They often refuse to accept the bare necessities of life; even if necessity drives them to accept a gift on occasion, they are content with getting their most precious needs satisfied, although many people are willing to give them much more than that. (*Contra Celsum* 3.9)

But this informal spontaneity of volunteers served not only as the exemplary precedent but also as a contributing factor to the network of congregations taking root around the empire. Except for Judaism, none of the other religions or philosophies had anything comparable to the unity of teaching and practice of Christianity. Further, this growing network of Christian churches provided a basic logistical blessing for missionaries—it was a built-in hospice program, providing a welcome with room and board for those who, with divine urgency, had left everything behind.

In earliest church history the wandering Christian missionaries went first to synagogues to win adherents. The Jews in the synagogues were used to new teachings; it was not unusual for new denominations to develop within Judaism. What was unique was that such a group would grow larger than the original body, as happened with Christianity. In the end, this would cause difficulties.

Since a Jewish appeal to Greeks had been developing within Judaism of the first century AD, Christianity was seen as competition by those who supported Jewish outreach to gentiles. But what was it that gave the victory to Christianity?

The common explanation is that the Christian defection from the Maccabean revolt against Rome in AD 70 severed Jewish-Christian ties. When it looked as if the Roman soldiers would invade Jerusalem and punish

Jews for their military rebellion, Christians left the city. This loss of manpower enraged the Jewish leaders. Christians remembered Jesus' advice to flee when they knew the final battle was near.

However, there is a more far reaching explanation for the wide gulf that developed between Jews and Christians. Some have observed that within Judaism there had been a growing division over outreach to gentiles, something to which the Christians following Jesus' commission were fully committed.

Near the end of the first century rabbis committed to more traditionally Jewish ways were increasing in importance. They emphasized the *Talmud,* an explication of Jewish law. "Talmudic" Judaism challenged and eventually displaced those who wanted to shape a Judaism acceptable to the gentiles. Up to this time many gentiles had associated themselves with synagogues, but according to Glenn Hinson, "This was a fatal choice."

Talmudic Judaism had an inherent nationalism, "strangeness of observance," and lacked a "mystical element."[43] The force to remain a separate Jewish community apart from the culture became dominant. The result was the end of mission outreach to the Jews.

The success of Christian outreach to the gentiles is what finally caused a separation between Jews and Christians. An urgency for mission caused the churches of Christ to break out of their former Jewish mold and instead shape their life and teaching for gentiles. Who caused this? Was this Paul's doing?

The outreach to the gentiles occurred so early in the church's history that it must, as Latourette suggests, be traced to Jesus. The preaching to gentiles and the jettisoning of Jewish ceremony happened too soon in church history to be the influence of anyone else.

By the end of the first century there was a Christian network of congregations which gave support to the Christian missionaries. As the network of churches grew so did the need for coordination. Able leaders in the form of capable administrators played more of a role in mission growth after the second century.

From his point of view, a critical Gibbon suggested five causes for Christian success in missions:

1. Intolerant zeal derived from the Jewish mission.
2. Emphasis on eternal tortures for those who did not repent.
3. The miracles and the "awful ceremony" of exorcism.
4. The "serious and sequestered life."
5. The government of the church, with its "scope for ambition and authority."[44]

At times we undervalue the role of church administration, but historically the growth of the church has been helped by an able church leadership.

To recap, in early church history there appear to be three stages of growth for the church.[45] The first was during the generation after Jesus, the so-called "apostolic age." During this time Christianity took in Jews and gentiles associated with Jews.

The second stage was from the last part of the first century to the close of the second century. Not many Jews were converted but the faith spread among the gentiles.

The third stage was from AD 180 to the time of Emperor Constantine. After Emperor Marcus Aurelius died and Commodias had assumed office, the Roman Empire was torn by internal strife, disease and war. As the institutions of the empire were weakened, Christianity won many new converts. The growth of the church picked up momentum. Especially so because the churches that were being planted had exceptional leadership and were outreach oriented.

Christians carried the message throughout the known world. One contributing factor was the written word. Christians preferred the *codex* (book) for the sacred texts while the pagans still utilized the roll. Made of papyrus, not parchment, the book was more compact, thus easier to take on a journey. It was more suited for a people on the move.[46]

Christianity expanded initially along the trade routes - so cities became the first home for the new faith, carried there by Jewish, Greek and Syrian business people. According to Robin Fox, by the mid-third century Christianity was present in towns and cities of every description, and "its gospels ... were preached in the major literary languages ...."[47]

Expansion of the church is also evidenced by larger meetings that took place. For example, a Synod in Rome in AD 251 was attended by sixty Italian bishops. By AD 300 Jesus' word was being proclaimed in all the known world. That there were Christians in Britain, can be seen from the fact that bishops from London, York and Colchester attended the Synod of Arles in AD 314. The church was expanding, and doing so without people who were called *apostles*. But we might stop and ask, "Who it was that carried their authority?"

When a local church was founded by one of the original Apostles, the Apostle presided at the first communion services and performed the first baptisms. But there came a time when the Apostle would leave; who took over?

Further, we know that not all churches were founded by one of The Twelve. We are in the ecclesiastical dark as to who founded the churches in Colossae, Laodicea, Philadelphia, Smyrna and Alexandria. We are not even told who began the most important gentile church, the one in Antioch, nor do we know who it was that founded the church in Rome. It is fair, however, to assume that in neither case was one of the Twelve Apostles involved.

Even *apostles* (in the broad sense) began to become associated with the past; missionary work was done less and less by commissioned workers and more and more by individual Christians as they lived their daily lives in love, hope, joy and with exemplary morality. Apostles *per se* disappeared. Still, as one would expect there came a time when a more authoritative office was needed.

When The Twelve founded churches they raised up local leaders called *presbyters* who assumed authority once the Apostle moved on. Among other things these "elders" had responsibility for teaching accurately the doctrines passed on to them. But at the same time there also existed another ministry which had authority, one that was not tied to one location, as the presbyter's ministry was.

In the second century, Christian communities were founded by itinerant missionaries, people who do not appear to have been authorized by any person or community. Many Christians became unwittingly *itinerant* out of sheer necessity—to flee for their own lives from persecution. The Lord used such eruptions of Satan's attacks to ultimate good—church expansion.

This seems to be the case in the early Christian document *The Works of Paul and Thecla* and in Clement of Rome's *Homilies* and *Recognitions*. Clement was a disciple of Peter and Paul and was bishop of Rome from AD 92 until 101. These missionaries were not "elected" by the church, such as those in the settled ministries, the presbyters. They felt called to the work by God. And they were honored, were to be given "the firstfruits of the wine press and the threshing floor, and of the cattle and sheep."[48]

These ministers may not have been formally authorized by an ecclesiastical body, but they understood themselves to have authority. They were ministers in the apostolic church, the church that had been sent by Christ. They did not stay long in one place and were dedicated to poverty, living off the generosity of congregations.

There also were peripatetic prophets and apostles who moved from community to community not only to begin but to build up established congregations. By the end of the first century charlatans infiltrated these mobile ministers, as attested to in the *Didache* (*Teaching of The Twelve Apostles*).

The *Didache* (*Teaching*), written sometime in the late first or early second century, was used to prepare a new Christian for baptism. The first part of this manual (the first six sections) are focused on moral issues. The second half instructs baptismal candidates regarding baptism, prayers, holy communion and offices in the church.

In the second part of the Didache there is a warning given to be on the lookout for false apostles. In the eleventh chapter (v 4) the manual says, "Let every apostle who comes to you be welcomed as if he were the Lord." This would have made sense to people who understood the Jewish apostle. ("The messenger of a man is as the man himself.") In this way the Christian *apostle,* both in the narrow *and the broad sense,* was the authoritative re-presentation of Jesus. But there was trouble beginning.

Verses five and six instruct,

> But he [the apostle in the broad sense] is not to stay for more than one day, unless there is need, in which case he may stay another. But if he stays three days, he is a false prophet. And when the apostle leaves, he is to take nothing except bread until he finds his next nights's lodging. But if he asks for money, he is a false prophet.[49]

The title *apostle* is beginning to fall into disrepute, it is beginning to mean "charlatan," or "swindler." In *Didache* 11.12, the warning is given,

> If anyone should say in the spirit, "Give me money," or anything else, do not listen to him. But if he tells you to give on behalf of others who are in need, let no one judge him.

There were some who were claiming to be apostles who were out for their own gain, contrary to Jesus' commission to his apostles in Matthew 10:9. Paul the Apostle infers the same thing in Philippians 1:15-18. But there was another reason to move away from the title *apostle.*

If indeed the missionaries of the Gnostics were called *apostles* then the early church would have preferred to find a different term.

It became obvious that the Gnostics were not going to see the Christian light, that they would continue to see their image of the Savior and their interpretation of Jesus apart from the public witness of The Twelve apostles. The challenge the church gave to the Gnostic leaders was this: "If your understanding of the Christ is accurate, why not share it publicly?" Why should one have to learn in secret the knowledge that brings life? Share the Good News openly! Share the way to salvation for free, do not make people pay to learn what God has freely offered to all.

It is in this context that the word apostle falls into disuse by Christian churches. But what would take its place?

In his monumental work *A History of the Expansion of Christianity,* Kenneth Scott Latourette wrote, "When the office of bishop arose, one of its functions seems to have been winning pagans to the faith."[50] By AD 150 bishops were taking the leading role in spreading the faith. It was they who received the authorization and used it to bring Christ to others.

At times a bishop or group of bishops would authorize another bishop to begin a new mission. Phaedimus of Anasae was authorized by Gregory and sent to Neocasearea. Eusebius of Nicomedia along with other bishops consecrated Ulfilas in AD 341 and sent him to work among the Goths. But bishops also sent others who were not bishops to begin new churches.

Deacons and presbyters also began new mission fields. In the late second and early third centuries Lyons was the center of mission work in Gaul. In the *Letter of the Churches of Lyons and Vienna*, a deacon is described as leading the church at Vienna. Further,

> Irenaeus sent the presbyter Ferreal and the deacon Ferjeux to found a church in Besancon and the presbyter Felix and the two deacons Achilles and Fortunatus to found one in Valence.[51]

Another strategy was for the bishop himself to meet with a new group that had already been established. Later they would elect a presbyter who would then be ordained. According to Glenn Hinson, Gregory of Thaumaturgas went to Comance, taught for a long time and then consecrated a man from the area by the name of Alexander as their bishop.

And a bishop might decide to go into a new mission field and by himself evangelize people with the intention of starting one or more congregations. He would then prepare a suitable candidate to continue the work after him. Hinson says this is what happened in Ireland.

Even as late as the fourth century Patrick acted as an

> itinerant metropolitan with no fixed see. He envisioned God's appointment of him as a general commission, "that through me many people should be regenerated to God and afterwards confirmed,' and that clergy should everywhere be ordained for them ....[52]

In essence, the bishop is continuing the work of the apostle as missionary. This particular strategy was more common than some bishops of today want to admit.

Back in the third century Origen knew of workers who specifically did mission outreach and were actually called *bishops*. These were the "country bishops." One council compared them to the seventy disciples of Jesus "because they serve the poor."[53] Their work was concentrated in the poorer places, in the villages of rural areas. They themselves remained poor and travelled with few possessions.

These committed missionaries went from village to village evangelizing, starting new congregations and educating leaders for the new groups. In New Testament days workers such as these could have been called *apostles*. In fact the name *apostle* did continue.

In tradition, St. Gall is known as the apostle of northeastern Switzerland; Willibrord became the apostle of the Frisians (what is today Holland) and Boniface, who lived in the seventh and eighth centuries, became illustrious as the apostle to the Germans. Much in mission was accomplished by individuals working in the apostolic way, but the major paradigm for mission outreach centered on one particular group: the local congregation.

By the end of the second century public mission preaching was outmoded. The practice of Christian missionaries entering a town and beginning their work by preaching in the local synagogue was discontinued. In its place there was a system of instruction and nurture found in local congregations. The congregation became the major strategy for missionary work. This marks an advance which lasted for centuries.

Most people brought to Christ came initially through the attractiveness of the exemplary lives of the people of God. There were various things that made Christianity appealing: the promise of forgiveness for sins, miracles, exorcisms, the claim to be the "ancient people of God," promises of immortality and escape from eternal punishment, and love for the poor.[54] In Christians people saw a counterculture, something different, something they wanted for themselves.

The Christian difference was most evident in the moral commitment of Jesus' followers. The willingness to forgive an enemy and their love for the outcast made a deep impression on non-Christians. Christianity taught the spiritual worth of the poor, and in particular the worth of those cast aside by society.

As far back as the second century AD, charity occupied a significant place in the ministry of congregations. According to Justin (d. 165), "We who formerly loved money and property more than anything else now place what we have in the common fund and share with everyone in need."[55] The community held a common treasury into which contributions were place to support the poor, the aged, slaves, "shipwrecked persons, and any persons who are in the mines, on islands or in prisons because of their Christian confession."[56]

To say the church was "catholic" was not just to say it extended all over the world but that it extended to all classes of people. Through the centuries this remained true. "Julian observed (fourth century) that 'there were members in the Christian churches whom no other religious societies would tolerate within their bounds."[57]

Celsus, a leader of the anti-Christian forces, writing in AD 278, suggested derisively that Christians never entered into conversations with intelligent pagans but instead made their appeal to adolescents, crowds of slaves and fools. Still the Christian appeal won the hearts of all levels of people. Why? The willingness of Christian people to give up their lives as martyrs rather than give up their faith lent credibility to their witness. In general, Christians were convinced that the Day of Judgement was very near and that they were "debtors to the heathen."[58]

After having been attracted to the faith, potential adherents were invited to begin preparation for complete membership; it was then that teachers and preachers presented a forceful argument for the doctrine of Christ. Once admitted, the new convert could expect moral and spiritual support from the congregation to live out their new nature in Christ.

The work of the church included both outreach and inreach. Those within the community were instructed and disciplined in the faith. Christianity was unique in that it included in its education unlearned and simple men.

To learn philosophy these people would have needed money and the means to migrate to Alexandria. But to learn the Christian faith, all they had to do was to go to their church. There the presbyter preached for no fee; and above him was a learned bishop, who would also occasionally be present to share insights on the Christian teaching. In this way Christianity grabbed hold of the entire person, their thoughts, their feelings and their actions. Ultimately this is what assured its victory. Not individuals, but an entire system of organized individuals, all available in the local church, is what won the soul of the Roman Empire. The difference can be summed up by saying that while pagans won adherents, Christianity was organized to win converts.

The process of persuasion was detailed, it was long and hard. As part of the process each church developed a creed (from the Latin *credo*, "I believe").

The local Christian community's creed provided the outline for instruction, particularly for those preparing for baptism. In effect the creed served a mission function. Irenaeus' creed of AD 180 even included a statement of mission:

> and to raise up all flesh of all mankind, that, according to the good pleasure of the Father invisible, every knee of those that are in heaven and on the earth and under the earth should bow before Christ Jesus, our Lord and God and Savior and King, and that every tongue should confess to him, and that he may execute righteous judgment over all ….

Sometimes the creed was called a *symbol.* The word comes from the Greek, meaning "to throw together" or "to compare." Cyprian in about AD 250 was the first to use *symbol* in a theological sense. In the fourth century it became a common word for a statement of faith.

The use of the creed was to change under Constantine. In this emperor's administration it was against the law to be a heretic. A way was needed to tell orthodox (correct) Christians from those holding aberrations of the Christian faith. It was the creed which was enlisted for this role.

The creed in the fourth century began to be used as a military password since Christians regarded themselves as soldiers of Christ fighting under the banner of the cross.[59] Finally this would cause a change in the function

of the creed from a missionary use to a tool for conservation of the faith
and the faithful.

Before Constantine each community would adopt its own summary of
belief, with the only regularity being incorporation of the three articles:
since Jesus (Mt 28) had commissioned his disciples to baptize the peoples
of the world "In the Name of the Father, and of the Son and of the Holy
Spirit," statements of belief about each member of the Trinity formed the
outline for teaching.

The investment of time and effort paid off as evidenced by the superior
level of commitment of those brought to Christ. This was happening even as
the motive for mission was changing.

At first Christians were motivated by urgent concerns to reach all people
before Jesus' return. However, as time went by expectation of an immediate
return of Jesus diminished. As has been noted, the first century document
Didache demonstrates this change.

Robert Grant, prominent historian of the New Testament era, also
noticed a difference between the prayers of the Didache and those of the later
1 Clement. In the *Didache* Christians gave thanks for God's gifts and prayed
for the deliverance of the church into God's kingdom. The prayer is "Let
grace come and let this world pass away."[60] The end of the world is near. But
Clement's prayer, according to Hinson, another historian of the early church,
is for peace in this world, for health and security, for the rulers of the world,
whom God has placed in authority. This is evidence of a church accommo-
dating itself to the present world. And there is more such evidence.

In the third century, as Grant points out, "At baptism one tasted milk and
honey as symbols of an entrance into the land of promise already made."[61] In
other words, the anticipation of the coming kingdom of God was lessened,
and entering the body of Christ at baptism was understood as the time of
entrance into the "promised land." The emphasis was this: eternal life begins
now. We do not sit around and wait for the Lord to return and bring us into
the next life. Life on earth is a participation in eternal things—when we live
in the forgiveness of sins, when we share in the body and blood of the Lord
Jesus, when we practice forgiveness and charity, we show we are already living in the kingdom which has not yet fully come.

The point is, the Church's reason to do missions was changing. Another
reason was added.

At first it had been the urgency to get the word out before Christ
returned. Now there was also the motive of Christian exclusiveness. "There is
no salvation outside of the church" writes Cyprian. Christianity could tolerate
no competitors. Worship of the time reinforced this understanding, particularly in the eating of the Lord's supper.

The holy communion was celebrated in secret, and only Christians were allowed to participate. This heightened the sense of Christianity's exclusivity. The procedures for entry into the church impressed upon everyone the claim of absoluteness of the faith. This created for many a perception of a "bigoted outlook, which inflamed a zeal to win everyone to the one true religion."[62]

Acts 4:12 demands a certain kind of exclusivity - but an exclusivity intended for all! The danger now was to move from an urgency to tell the Good News because Christ was coming soon, to an extreme emphasis that we are right, everyone else wrong, and our zeal is inflamed to help them know the truth so they can be saved.

This change in emphasis did not curb fearless Christian witness. Eusebius tells us that Christianity began in Georgia through a woman. Nina (or Nona) had been captured in war, but did not allow that to annul her faith. Through her influence a church building was constructed. But another witness was more compelling: martyrdom.

God has marvelous ways of turning Satan's strategy to destroy the church into ultimate good. Thus, even martyrdom became one of the most public announcements for Christianity. Even though martyrdoms were relatively rare for most of Church history, when they did occur they won people to Christ. At least that is what we are told by one of the early Christian writers, Tertullian.

Tertullian was born about AD 160, the child of a pagan centurion. He studied public speaking and law, and was won to Christianity when he was about thirty years old. Until his defection to one of the many heresies of the late second century, he was a powerful proponent of Christianity.

It was Tertullian who observed that when Christians were brought to die in the arena the crowds would shout, "Look how these Christians love one another." Christian love under persecution made a deep impression, even on persecutors. It played a part in bringing many to faith in Christ. But Tertullian wasn't the only witness to the positive effects of Christian martyrdom.

In this same period a philosopher by the name of Justin had been studying the works of Plato. He had heard about Christians, heard that they were immoral and loved pleasure more than knowledge. But Justin says that when he observed how Christians would die "without fear" as martyrs, he knew the accusations against them were lies. He came to realize that they despised death because of their deep commitment to the truth. These were people who were not in love with the world, but were deeply committed to loving others. These were people he wanted to join.

We have looked at the place of the church in the Roman Empire in the second and third centuries and how the church was apostolic in that time. This was the time when mission work moved away from being the responsibility of particular individuals to something the church, especially the local church, carried out.

It was also a time in which the focus of the church broadened so that there was a shift from concentrating on an initial urgency simply to get the Gospel out to the whole world before Christ returned, to include also the need to share and confess what Christians believed to be the only true way into eternal life. Because of heresies that arose their confessional defense of the Gospel was necessary (Acts 4:12; 1 Pet 3:15-17). This could well have been one of the influencing factors that caused the term *apostolic church* to be perceived as the church which confesses the teaching of the apostles at the expense of the other inherent part of its meaning, (i.e., "the church that is sent").

Chapter 7
Recovering the Full Meaning of Apostolic

In the New Testament there were two "essential" qualities for apostles, having seen the risen Christ and having been commissioned. But two other characteristics seem also to have been important: poverty and indefatigable missionary activity.[63] This continued through the first century, when congregations were being planted in all parts of the world. As John Burnaby has pointed out, apostolic was an adjective first applied to particular churches whose tradition claimed that they had been founded by an apostle or apostles. It signaled a continuity of the church in time and in understanding.

And, from the second century on, stress was laid on the bishop as the evidence of this continuity. The bishop came to symbolize the apostolic nature of the church. his authority, rested on an "unbroken chain of succession from the apostles or 'apostolic men' who founded the church over which he presided."[64]

Near the end of the first century apostles came under suspicion because of the abuse of the office by charlatans (cf. Phil 1:15-16). While the *Didache* treats apostles with respect, when it discusses this ministry, it is primarily interested in laying down rules to prevent exploitation by impostors, people who are becoming a nuisance to the Christian communities. In fact, the *Didache* stands at a turning point in church organization.[65]

The author of the *Didache* instructed the congregations to appoint bishops, overseers of life and doctrine, and deacons, ministers who serve the Lord. These workers would continue in one location the work of the apostles and prophets who moved from place to place. The situation is fluid.

The apostles and prophets still have authority, but this authority was to be shared with local leadership. The writer of the *Didache* still expected the momentary arrival of Jesus, so there is not much concern for how people will succeed to office. The situation changes again in Clement's letter.

In *1 Clement* 42.1-4, *apostles* are in the past. God sent Christ, who sent apostles, who established bishops and deacons. Because of the growth of the church more attention was being paid to organizing an institution than to outreach. Not at this time but later, in Origen's day, *apostle* came to refer to The Twelve only.

It was believed that the apostles' task had been to bring the Gospel to the whole world, which, it was assumed, they had. Missionaries, therefore, could not be called apostles, because "they were no longer the first to preach the Gospel to the nations."[66]

The word *apostolic* does not appear in Christian writing until around AD 110, in Ignatius' letter to the Trallean church. As has already been noted, Ignatius used the word to describe the form of his letter, although it is conceivable this bishop on his way to martyrdom was also claiming a closer connection with the Trallean community. Was he its founder?

Another early use of the word *apostolic* is found in the writings of Clement of Alexandria. Near the end of the second century Clement was head of the "adult education department" at the Christian school in Alexandria. Previously, he had been a pagan philosopher, but had come to faith in Christ. Origen was one of his star pupils.

For Clement of Alexandria, Clement of Rome (who lived at the end of the first century) was an *apostle*.[67] But this reference is probably to Clement of Rome's sound teaching, not his missionary work. In Book Seven of the *Stromata* (ch. 16) the word *apostolic* is used in the same way: "maintaining apostolic and ecclesiastic orthodoxy." His pupil retained that emphasis.

Origen was a deeply committed Christian. Born in Alexandria of Christian parents about AD 185, he taught in school and instructed converts to the Christian faith. His burning love for the Lord caused him to go to great lengths, although some thought he went too far.

In the nineteenth chapter of Matthew, Jesus instructed his disciples about marriage, warning them of the requirement to remain with one spouse. After his strict teaching the disciples asked him if it was even worth it to get married. Jesus responded,

> Not everyone can accept this word, but only those to whom it has been given. For some are eunuchs because they were born that way; others were made that way by men; and others have renounced marriage because of the kingdom of heaven. (Mt 19:11-12)

Origen's zeal moved him to become physically one of the latter.

Origen understood the word *apostolic* to refer to correct teaching. In the Preface to his major work *De Principiis* (ch. 2) he wrote,

> The teaching of the church transmitted in orderly succession from the apostles, and remaining in the churches to the present day, is still preserved; that alone is to be accepted as truth which differs in no respect from ecclesiastical and apostolic tradition.

An older contemporary of Origen, Bishop Irenaeus of Lyons, held similar views. Irenaeus, "The Peaceful", was born in Smyrna, modern day Izmir (it is in Ignatius' letter to the Smyrnaens that the word *catholic* is first used; Ignatius was good at coining new theological words).

For Irenaeus, the apostles were not primarily missionaries, but teachers, who had transmitted their doctrines to the bishops; specifically, to Linus at Rome, and at Smyrna to Polycarp. Only what was apostolic was orthodox, and it was the bishop who inherited the mantle of the apostle.

For many today this is still the primary work of a bishop. The word *apostolic*, born with missionary blood in its veins, is not thought of in a missionary sense. It has lived its life as a twin of the proper but more narrow word *orthodox*. But now is the time for a recovery of the full meaning of *apostolic*; now is the time for *apostolic* to become reacquainted with another sibling, the word *missionary*.

It was in the second and third centuries that the church itself became truly apostolic, that is, missionary. As I have shown, it was not professional missionaries that were the most effective heralds of the Gospel, but congregations and individual believers. However, the term *apostolic church* is not used before the fourth century.

Where did the name come from? The first use of *apostolic church* is not in the Creed adopted at Nicea; in fact, the phrase was not originally in that creed! Where did it come from? When did it become a part of the Nicene Creed?

Part IV
"As an undiminished flow of water."

– Theodore of Mopsuestia describing the
Holy Spirit in the Nicene Creed, (ca. AD 400)

When the Emperor, dressed in his royal purple robes, entered the inner judgement hall of the imperial palace the Council of Nicea was ready to begin. Some who saw him thought Constantine was the epiphany prayed for by Christians all over the empire. Three centuries of waiting were now over—surely these must be the last days prophesied by Jesus. God's kingdom had come to earth; a Christian was now ruler of the Roman Empire. The year was AD 325 and Emperor Constantine's entrance signalled the beginning of the first empire-wide Christian assembly.

The council was called to bring unity to the church, and thus to the empire. But the question remains, "How is the phrase *apostolic church* understood in the Nicene Creed?" "What might this mean for the church today?"

Chapter 8
Constantine and Rome Before Nicea

The time was ripe for a new religion in the Roman Empire. In the decades before Constantine came to power, less and less attention was paid to the Roman gods. Near the end only the emperors were concerned with maintaining the old gods, and that only because those divinities were regarded as protectors of the empire. The people, however, were no longer looking for that protection.

Society was disintegrating as old ties between people and the gods of Rome were being broken down. The cities were filled with thousands who had been separated voluntarily or by force from their homes. Chief among these were slaves and merchants.[68] Seeking a place to belong, these people were drawn to Christianity by the strong organization of its churches in the present world, and by the security promised for the next life.

The church as a closely knit community included all races and classes; it welcomed men and women, rich and poor. This closeness provided "community" for people fragmented in their relationships. Works of love displayed Christian integrity to all. Charity was at the heart of the local congregation, and the church never sought to take revenge on its enemies. Christian people demonstrated their beliefs in their daily lives. Church teaching was simple enough for the unlearned, but profound enough to attract the most intellectual.

Concerning its central doctrines Christianity was inflexible; to join, a person had to make a break with the culture. But in its practice the church was flexible.[69]

Furthermore, the Romans believed in demons while Christianity claimed and demonstrated the power to expel demons. Christians insisted that Jesus' continued presence within the church is what gave her power and success in all she did.

For all these reasons, Latourette says that by the time of Constantine the church had become the most important internal rival of the state, and "next to the state the most powerful institution in the Empire."[70]

Constantine started his rise to become sole monarch of the Roman empire in the year AD 312. It was then that he left Gaul and moved against

Maxentius, the *de facto* ruler of Italy. He shivered across the alps with a small army to attack Maxentius who was dug in at Rome. It was a daring move. Only five years before, another army had come up against Maxentius and had failed to breach Rome's massive walls. This time things would turn out differently. Constantine was sure he would prevail because he had been given a sign from heaven.

The future emperor believed he needed divine intervention; he was certain that Maxentius was casting pagan spells and proffering sacrifices to ensure victory. Significantly Constantine did not look for help from the old Roman gods. He was in search of a "supreme god" who had appeared to his father, Constantius.

Constantius claimed to have received help from this god, and Constantine believed it. While the followers of the old gods were coming to terrible ends, his father had died a natural death. Not knowing who this god was, Constantine was praying for him to reveal himself. And that is when it happened.

There are two witnesses who recorded Constantine's account of the vision seen by him and his troops: Lactantius and Eusebius. Lactantius was the first to tell the story, writing within four years of the vision. Lactantius became the tutor of Constantine's son and gives the most detail. According to the tutor, Constantine had sworn he had a dream the night before the battle in which he was ordered to draw the "heavenly sign of God" on his soldiers' shields.[71] The sign he saw was a cross with a *chi rho* at its top.

Eusebius gives us the other account, taken from a sworn statement of Constantine. Writing twelve years after Constantine's death Eusebius says that not only Constantine but also all of his troops saw the sign in the noonday sky, accompanied by the words *IN HOC SIGNO VINCES* (in this sign you will conquer). That night, according to Eusebius, Christ came to him in a dream carrying the symbol they had seen earlier, and ordered the warrior to "use its likeness in his engagements with the enemy."[72] When he woke up the next morning, Constantine told others his dream and began to create a standard that would be topped with the *chi rho* letters supported by a cross. What many do not realize is that the symbol was not unique.

The Greek letter *chi* is the first letter in Christ, and *rho* is the first letter in *rex* (king). For the church the symbol meant "Christ the King," a daring confession given the absolute leadership of the Roman monarch. According to Robin Fox, the *chi rho* symbol was not used by Christians before Constantine, but it was familiar to scholars. In pagan papyri it was used as a sign to mark "good" or "useful" passages![73]

In AD 312, to the surprise of everyone, Maxentius and his army came out from behind the walls of Rome to fight Constantine's army, and Maxentius was defeated. We do not know what made him leave a bastion which had given him the victory before, but Constantine understood this was the hand of the God who had revealed himself to help him. His prayers were answered: he had come upon that unknown God served by Constantius, his father.

Constantine's victory over Maxentius meant the beginning of many benefits for the church. In fact, never again would Christians gain so much from a military victory. Already in AD 313 Constantine began to share his wealth with Christian leaders; he sent financial help to the bishop of Carthage, to be distributed to persons named on a list brought by Ossius, the bishop of Cordova in southern Spain. But as magnificent as his gifts of money would be, Constantine had something much more important to contribute: his blessing.

In AD 313 the emperor proclaimed freedom for all religions. At the same time, all property which had been confiscated from Christian churches was to be restored; the government treasury would pay back those who had already bought church lands.[74] But as beneficent as Constantine felt towards his new found faith, he now received his first taste of the brokenness of the body of Christ.

The emperor had assumed that there was only one Christianity; when he found out that there were divisions in the church he changed his order so that only "catholic" Christians could receive retribution. Leaders of fringe groups who might cause trouble were to be brought in front of Roman courts.

This intervention of the government on behalf of the orthodox church was very new. The schismatic Donatus was moved to ask, "What has the emperor to do with the church?" The world was changing for the good of orthodox Christians.

In fact, Constantine now understood his role as that of a bishop. Speaking to the leaders of the church he said, "You are bishops of those inside the church while I have been appointed by God as bishop of those outside."[75] Traditionally in league with the leadership of the pagan religion, this first of the Christian emperors was ready to fill a similar position for the new faith. At times his church responsibilities were more of a burden than his responsibilities to the civil government.

Constantine understood himself to be "the servant of God," answerable to God for peace and unity in the church. He was genuinely afraid of God's anger against him if he failed to maintain concord. "As Emperor he was deeply concerned for Christian harmony, fearing that discord might annoy God."[76] Painfully, he learned that not even the power of the state could insure tranquility in the church. For one thing, the emperor was never able to bring the Donatists into line.

The Donatists taught a rigid Christianity that would not permit forgiveness for a lapse in faith, even a lapse under persecution. When the church catholic permitted pastors who under torture denied the faith to once again baptize and celebrate communion, the Donatists declared only themselves to be the true church, and broke off relations with the catholics.

Constantine, in an effort to bring the Donatists back into union with traditional Christians, began a state persecution of these rebels; but the Donatists held that persecution was a sign of the true church! Constantine was the first emperor to use force to try and heal a schism in the church and he was not successful. Most unfortunately, that did not keep him from trying.

One of the motivations for Constantine to win the Eastern part of the empire was to bring unity to the church. Battle successes between July and September AD 324 put Constantine on the throne of a united Roman empire. In a letter to the citizens of the eastern provinces he wrote that he desired "peace, concord, and tranquillity to be ensured by equal privileges for pagans and Christians alike". Christianity alone was the true religion, but in his prayers he asked God to allow the pagans to also enjoy his blessings.[77]

The support of the emperor, as welcome as it was, did not always bode well for the church. For decades the threat of persecution from outside had kept Christians united. Once the outside threat was removed, cracks appeared in Christian unity. Having failed to patch the fissures with threats and physical punishment, the emperor would ultimately turn to persuasion in the form of an empire-wide gathering.

The endorsement of the emperor created changes for the church, not the least of which was a favorable climate for evangelism. This did not start with Constantine; he, in part, was riding the crest of a Christian tidal wave that was inundating the world. But the emperor's conversion harnessed the wave's power, focussed and channeled it. Under Constantine the church grew from a sizable minority to become the majority religion. This brought other changes.

In the apostolic age Christians had lived as if Jesus would return at any moment; therefore earthly governments were ignored. There was no need to participate in something that was not going to be around very long and temporal power would not be needed in the new order. For that reason, there was also no need for Christians to rebel against the state, as Jewish revolutionaries were doing. In time this perspective changed.

The Christians of the early fourth century still were committed to the faith, but now Jesus' return did not seem so close. As evidence, Christ's followers were ready to accept Constantine's vision of an army led by the sign of the Savior. Before marching east against the Persians, Constantine asked the bishops at his court to accompany him. And when they consented, he is said to have revealed his battle plans to them. For many, God's kingdom had now come and Constantine was the deliverer.

What changes had occurred after three centuries! A religious movement which appeared in the eyes of the world to be an obscure sect of Judaism with no one of worldly power involved developed an extensive organization second only to that of the empire, in time becoming the one religion of that empire. Jesus' followers came to hold the allegiance of the vast majority of the population in the Mediterranean basin, and that allegiance continued after the empire's demise.[78]

Chapter 9
The First Council of Nicea (325)

But the weight of disunity in the church continued to be a difficult burden for Constantine. He had tried by force to unite the Christian factions and was not successful. The goal was too important to be discarded so the emperor searched for other means of conciliation. If only those who disagreed could talk about their differences, maybe then peace in the church could be won. An intelligent leader, he considered himself a forceful person and persuasive enough to win over all antagonists.

The biggest disagreements centered around Arius, a presbyter who questioned the divine nature of Jesus. The debate began in AD 318 when Arius was a priest in Baucalis. In Arius' words,

> We are persecuted because we say the Son hath a beginning, but God hath no beginning. Because of this we are persecuted, and because we say he is from things which are not; for so we say, because he is not a part of God, nor yet from any presupposed thing.[79]

In more modern terms, Arius taught that God was not created, Jesus was created, therefore Jesus could not be God.

The opposition to Arius was led by a deacon by the name of Athanasius. For Athanasius, Jesus had to have been God because "Only a Being himself of the essence of God could unite God and man."[80] The deacon confronted the presbyter with passages such as John 1:1, "In the beginning was the Word and the Word was with God and the Word was God." Athanasius' theology was closest to the theology of the Western church. Bishop Ossios, Constantine's spiritual advisor, was from the West. Ossios convinced Constantine that to unite the traditions of the Eastern and Western churches Constantine should support Athanasius.[81]

Besides the dispute with Arius, the council would address other factors causing division: it would consider setting a common date to celebrate Easter, and such a council could discuss the problem of discipline after sin. Besides this there was the need to celebrate peace in the empire and to give thanks for the triumph of Christianity.

In order to bring everyone together in one place, Constantine planned and paid for the first ecumenical (empire-wide) church council. Originally the council was to meet in Ancyra (in modern day Turkey) but for the sake of accessibility and better climate it was moved. The meeting would be held at the emperor's residence near Nicomedia, the capital of the Roman Empire in AD 325.

In the 280's the emperors were busy with military threats from the East. To be closer to the action, they developed a city in the East as a capital. That city was Nicomedia, in the Roman province of Bithynia. Nicea, thirty miles south of Nicomedia, is where the emperor's palace was located.

Nicea was also an important city in Bithynia. Because of its location on the busy trade routes through Bithynia it had become a significant center of commerce and culture. It is described as "a charming lake side city," with a good climate.[82] Bithynia also played a role in Christian history: it is the area from which Paul was kept by the Spirit of Christ (Acts 16:7). This city which had once represented a closed door to early Christian church planters would now become the site of the triumph of Christianity, and a wide open portal for church expansion.

The time for the meeting would be May and June of 325. Constantine paid the travel costs for the delegates, lodged them in his palace, fed them and gave them presents at the end of the meeting. Without the aid of this Christian emperor the council would have been virtually impossible; certainly it would never have had as significant an impact on the civil government.

This council was a necessary part of the evolution of Christianity into the religion of the state. First and foremost, Nicea made a statement to the effect that Christianity was the religion of the Roman emperor, who desired the unity of the church so that the church could unite the empire. The council was a showcase, a weather vane for those testing the winds of change. Cannily, the emperor was not insisting that everyone believe as he did, but he wanted his friends to know what his belief was. The end product of the Council of Nicea was to be a statement of belief, a creed which would explain the new faith to all within and without the church.

As has been noted, it was Constantine who made the preparations for the Council. On her own authority, the church could not have called this council. There were over two hundred and fifty representatives, according to Eusebius (Constantine says there were over three hundred). Staying in the emperor's palace they were surrounded with luxury. What a change it must have been for many who had suffered through state persecutions to now be feted by the state. One tradition says that a certain Paphnutios visited personally with Constantine. Paphnutios had been blinded in one eye during the persecution under Maximinius; in tears, the emperor is supposed to have bent over and kissed the blind eye.

The Council began on the first of June, 325. Of the more than two hundred and fifty bishops, only five were from the West. The bishop of Rome, Sylvester, did not attend because of his advanced age; in his place he sent two presbyters. Presiding over the Council was Ossius, a bishop of the West, from Cordova. The meetings of this, the first and most important of the four ecumenical councils would last for less than a month.

The opening of the Council of Nicea took place in the inner judgment hall of the royal palace. The Christian bishops sat in silence in rows parallel to the two long walls of the hall.[83] At the start the closest attendants of the Emperor, the Christian attendants, made their entrance. With a signal from the master of ceremonies all the delegates stood up and the Emperor himself appeared, "resplendent as one of God's angels in heaven."[84]

According to accounts of the time,

His purple mantle shone in the reflected light of shimmering gold and jeweled ornaments. With his eyes down, but with great dignity, he slowly stepped to his place in the front where there was a small gold armchair. But he did not sit down until the bishops signalled him and all the others to sit.[85]

He sat in isolation, although he joined in all of the discussions. Ossius may have been presiding but it was Constantine who was in control.

At the moment Constantine entered, the bishop leading the section on the right, Eusebius, stood up to express the thanks of the delegates to the Emperor. As bishop of the capital city Eusebius had that right. Constantine replied with only a few sentences, in which he said he hoped the victory won by military means over the tyrants would now be followed by victory over dissension within the church. He implored the delegates to become one in heart and in soul. His words were in Latin, to indicate this was an important moment for the empire, nevertheless, it seemed as if no one was listening to his wishes.

Immediately after the Council opened the charges began to fly. Countercharges were the response. Constantine was undeterred. Near the beginning of the Council the delegates had lined up in front of the emperor to fill his lap with petitions against each other—the emperor ordered the petitions burned. He joined in the debates, trying to guide the church to agreement. But in the end the major discussion took place concerning the adoption of a creed.

After Ossius introduced the topic of the creed, Constantine began the discussion with a few observations. It was Constantine who introduced the now famous word *homoousios*, ("of the same substance") to describe Jesus' relationship with the Father. In opposition to Arius this council would affirm that the Son was of the same substance with the Father. Some, such as Leitzmann, believe the word was a term used by laity who criticized clergy who had shown "Arian tendencies."

According to Eusebius, the template for the creed was the creed of the church in Caesarea. A coastal town in Palestine, Caesarea was the home of Cornelius, the Roman centurion, commander of the Italian regiment, whom Peter visited (Acts 10). It was in Cornelius' house that the church in Caesarea began; the first members were his family and friends. The lesson taught to Peter that day led to the acceptance of the gentiles into the church. Three centuries later the gift of that church was a common confession which would lead the empire to Christ. A Roman centurion had initiated a movement that would lead to a religious victory over the empire.

But there was still one more discovery even more interesting and certainly more pertinent than this. This time in church history the Arian controversy had taken center stage. For this reason, the intent of the Emperor (and those supporting the catholic interpretation) was to affirm that the Father and the Son were equally God (as opposed to the Arian understanding that the Father was before and superior to the Son). The Creed adopted in 325 fulfilled that intent. The articles on the Father and the Son made the confession that the two were "of the same substance." And the third article of the creed said simply "And we believe in the Holy Spirit." This in fact is how the creed of 325 ended.

The original intent of this study was to determine the meaning of the term *apostolic church* in the third article. However, research indicates that this term did not appear in the original version of the Nicene Creed.

On June 19, 325, after weeks of discussion, the Nicene Creed was signed. Ossius, who had been the first to announce the creed, was now the first to sign it. The Creed was then brought around to each attendee by Constantine's personal notaries, led by Philumenus, the "master of the offices".[86] Constantine was making sure he knew who was in his corner and who was not.

Finally, the Emperor addressed the delegates; he urged them to be friendly to each other and to keep the peace. By the end of the Council not all of the delegates had signed their names in agreement. However, shortly afterward, each attendee did sign, even though some had their own personal interpretation of what the words of the creed meant. In fact, two years later even Arius affixed *his* name to the creed, although he never admitted changing his mind.

No matter. Constantine got what he wanted, a creed by which to measure the faith of Christians in the empire. Those who subscribed to the creed were "catholic," orthodox Christians who confessed the faith as it had been believed in all times and all places. Those who would not subscribe were considered heretics. After the Council of Nicea heresy was against the law, punishable by forfeiture of property and deportation.

The Nicene Creed did not immediately replace the baptismal creeds which were used in local areas. It was a test of orthodoxy for bishops, not a tool of instruction for mission work. It was mainly used against the followers of Arius, to get them to conform to more traditional theology. Therefore, its major use was in the Eastern part of the empire; the church in the West was not much bothered with Arianism. However, the Nicene Creed is the only Creed to be officially adopted by both the Eastern and Western churches, and therefore the only truly ecumenical creed.

Under Constantine Christianity became the dominant religion of the empire, officially sanctioned and promoted by the Emperor. Many Christians saw the adoption of Christianity by the Emperor as realized eschatology, the kingdom of God had now arrived on earth. The sacrifices necessary in the past for spreading the Gospel were no longer necessary. Not only the laws but the riches of the empire were put at the church's disposal. Even with all that, Constantine was not able to put an end to the infighting among Christians. Philip Schaff tells the story of the Emperor's encounter with Acesius. Constantine urged Acesius, a Novatian bishop, to return to the catholic and apostolic church. The bishop replied that his separation was because the church no longer observed the ancient disciplines, which forbade those who had committed a mortal sin from ever being readmitted to communion. According to the Novatians such a sinner could repent, but the church could not assure them of forgiveness. That judgement was left to God.

It was then that Constantine said, "Acesius, take a ladder and climb up to heaven alone." These were words of frustration from a man who keenly desired a united church. The emperor usually got what he desired, but not in this case. The seer of visions, the lord of the most powerful of nations could not command church unity.

Constantine died on May 22, 337, Pentecost Sunday. In a cruel twist, Constantine's successor to the throne, his own son, Constantius, claimed to be a follower of Arius. After the death of his brothers Constantius was sole emperor for eleven years. During this time he persecuted those who held the Nicene faith.

Later, there would be others who denied the deity of the Holy Spirit. This is the issue that led to the second ecumenical council, and the adoption of the text we would recognize as the third article of the Nicene Creed.

Chapter 10
The First Council of Constantinople (381)

When did the term *apostolic church* become a part of the the Nicene Creed?

The First Council of Constantinople, held in AD 381 was the second of the empire-wide councils. The creed adopted at this council gave the church its "proper" names: holy, catholic and apostolic. Actually, these names were used in earlier creeds, but not together, and not in a creed adopted at an Ecumenical Council.

The term *apostolic* was first used by Ignatius in his letter to the Tralleans. Tralles was a very fertile area, described as the "orchard of Asia Minor."[87] It was a wealthy city. Tralles was the official residence of the Roman high priest, who in Ignatius' day lived in a palace. The civic leaders of Tralles were said to live in opulence. The president of the Roman games was expected to be someone of wealth, so consequently the person chosen was often from Tralles.

Tralles was on the high road between Laodicea and Ephesus; it is possible that Christianity was brought to this city by Paul himself. This is the church to which Ignatius writes "after the apostolic manner."

According to J.B. Lightfoot, by the close of the second century and the beginning of the third century, *apostolic* was a frequently used word. It was used to describe certain writings, as when Clement of Alexandria calls a passage from St. Paul "apostolic."[88] And in *Stromaties* 7.16, Clement talks about "*apostolic* and ecclesiatic salvation."

The term *holy church* had been used before, in Cyprian's Creed, around AD 250. The Apostles' Creed, as it appears in written form in the Greek about 340 is the first to use the phrase *catholic church* in a creed. And it appears that the Creed of Cyril of Jerusalem (about 350) is the first to confess faith in "one, holy, catholic church." But none of these had used the term *one, holy, catholic and apostolic*.

Origen, although never using the term *apostolic church* in his creed, in AD 230 did employ the phrase "The Father was the God of the apostles." Lucian's Creed from AD 300 ends with these words:

And in the Holy Ghost, given for consolation and sanctification
and perfection to those who believe; as also our Lord Jesus Christ
commanded his disciples, saying, "Go ye, teach all nations, baptizing them in the name of the Father, and of the Son, and of the
Holy Ghost."

Lucian also talks about Jesus being "The apostle of the Father."

The phrase *apostolic church* does not appear until the fourth century. It is
contained in a letter to Alexander of Constantinople written by Alexander of
Alexandria (d. 328). The first time the word appeared in a creed was in the
anathemas added to the body of the Nicene Creed in 325. But it is only with
the controversy over the divinity of the Holy Spirit that *apostolic church*
began to be used in the body of creeds.

It was not only the divinity of Jesus that was called into question;
whether the third person in the Trinity was equal to God was also questioned.
The fourth century commentator Theodore of Mopsuestia observed that even
though the Nicene Creed ended with "And in the Holy Spirit," later on,

Those who after them handed to us a complete doctrine concerning
the Holy Spirit were the Western bishops who by themselves assembled in a Synod, as they were unable to come to the East on account
of the persecution that the Arians afflicted on this country.[89]

Unfortunately, we do not have this confession.

There are, however, some who believe that the creed of Epiphanius
may reflect that lost creed. In any event, Epiphanius' Creed is the first
known instance of the term *apostolic church* being used in the body of a
Christian creed.

Epiphanius is known to history as "The learned champion of a narrow
and intolerant orthodoxy." And as "A well read man but narrow of mind and
obstinate." He was born in Palestine in the village of Besandus, near Gaza,
around AD 310, of Christian parents. It is said he was brought up in the faith
of Nicea. Educated by monks, Epiphanius completed his training for the
priesthood in Egypt.

A monk practically from childhood, he founded a monastery at
Eleytheropolis and served as its first abbot. He was very concerned about
keeping this monastery free from heresy. His reputation grew and in 367 he
was invited to the island of Cyprus to become the bishop of its capital,
Salamis. There he continued to be known for his austerity and zealous commitment to the truth. This reputation won for Epiphanius many adherents;
novices came to the monastery in Salamis from all over the known world.

In 374 Epiphanius wrote *The Anchored One*, a description of the "true
faith" for those tempted by the false doctrines of the day. Near the end of this

work he wrote, "The children of the church have received from the holy fathers, that is, from the holy apostles, the faith to keep, and to hand down, and to teach their children." He then goes on to quote a baptismal creed: "Which you and we and all the orthodox bishops of the whole catholic church together, make this address to those who come to baptism." This creed is almost identical with the creed we today call the Nicene Creed.

Pneumatomachian literally means in English "enemies of the spirit." It is the word used to refer to the followers of Apolinarius and Macedonius, both of whom denied that the Holy Spirit was fully God. Epiphanius' creed was probably the creed required of pneumatomachians converting from the fellowship of either of those two heretics. But Epiphanius only believed he was stating the faith of Nicea; the creeds do not contain any new teachings, only an expanded explanation in light of the new challenges to the orthodox faith.

Epiphanius died at sea in AD 403 on his way home from Constantinople, but his understanding of the Holy Spirit lived on. His creed became the basis of the belief adopted at the second ecumenical council, held in 381 in Constantinople.

Constantinople (present day Istanbul) occupied a strategic location at the entrance to the Black Sea. In that location it sat at the crossroads between Europe and Asia. The city was the brainchild of Constantine; in 324 he had decided to build a new capital city to replace the former capital, Nicomedia. Even though Constantine saw the city as the capital of the Roman empire, in time Constantinople would become the capital only for the Eastern part of the empire. Building for the city did not actually begin until AD 330.

The Council held there in 381 consisted of one hundred and fifty bishops, all from the East. It was not recognized as an "ecumenical" (empire-wide) council until the Council of Chalcedon (AD 451). The bishops had been called together at Constantinople by Emperor Theodosius to confront the Pneumatomachian issues. How would the church state its belief in a divine Trinity, affirming that Father, Son and Holy Spirit were all God? The Emperor desired to win over the Macedonians and Apolinarrians on the basis of the faith confessed at Nicea. The work of the Council went quickly.

The Council of Constantinople opened under the presidency of Meletius of Antioch, but Meletius died suddenly during the meeting. Gregory of Nazianzus was made Meletius' successor. Gregory, a talented theologian, was the oldest of three children born to the bishop of Nazianus. His mother, Nonna, consecrated him to church work before his birth. Gregory wanted to enter monastic life but his father insisted he had to work with him to check the Pneumatomachians in his district. Gregory's defense of Christian orthodoxy against Arius was very successful and finally his supporters forced him to accept the duties of bishop in Constantinople. Gregory would have preferred life in a monastery.

When Gregory was made president of the Council there was an uproar from his enemies. Rather than continue the fight he quit after only a few days in office. Nectarius took his place. After this the council's work progressed rapidly and a creed was adopted affirming faith in the Holy Spirit as equal to the Father and the Son. But then a curious thing happened. The creed was lost.

In the canons of the Council of Constantinople there is no creed. The Constantinopolitan Creed became generally known at the Council of Chalcedon. There a deacon from Constantinople, a man by the name of Aetius, read the creed to the assembled bishops of the fourth ecumenical council. Consensus immediately was reached that this indeed represented the Christian faith as it was taught all over the world. It represented the faith affirmed at Nicea, and was accepted as such. The delegates to Constantinople did not understand themselves to be creating a new faith or any new statement of faith. Some of the additions had been in use at least since AD 374. They only wanted to reaffirm the faith that had been taught by the apostles.

The Nicene/Constantinopolitan Creed took into account the "developments in doctrine, especially in regard to the Holy Spirit, which had taken place since Nicea."[90] Kelly believes that the creed adopted at Constantinople had started out as an attempt to placate the followers of the heretic Macedonius. However, the Macedonians finally rejected the new creed; the creed had lost its original purpose but was useful to the church in explaining the relationship and role of the third person in the Trinity, and so it was kept. In fact, the Constantinopolitan Creed is important because it affirmed for the first time the correctness of addressing prayers to the Holy Spirit.[91]

The Council of Trent adopted the Nicene/Constantinopolitan Creed as the chief creed of the Western Church. Since the Apostles' Creed was never officially accepted in the East,[92] the creed brought to life under Theodosius in 381 remains *the* ecumenical creed.

Chapter 11
The New Function of the Creed

Early on the creed was a mission tool. Creeds were used as both summaries and outlines for teaching the faith to new converts. But the Nicene and Nicene/Constantinopolitan creeds were adopted for different purposes.

Since Jesus had commanded baptism for all nations in the name of the Father, Son and Holy Spirit, creeds were originally written to teach the Trinity. Each local community of Christians might have its own creed, summarizing its teaching on the three persons. But the Christian mission challenge changed after Constantine, and along with it the function of a creed.

For one thing, the battle with evil became more focussed on social ills. For the first three centuries the mission was defined primarily in terms of evangelization, winning and incorporating new people into the body of Christ. After the emperor of Rome became a Christian the challenge became one of shaping society into the Christian ideal.[93] With the aid of the Emperor's riches Christian churches ministered to the sick, the poor and the elderly. In the late fourth century there were significant Christian hostels and charitable centers all over the empire. Constantine drew up legislation curbing the gladiatorial games and discontinued imperial support for them. Eventually those games would die out.

Christian charity became the primary Christian witness. Aid was given to everyone, Christian and pagan alike. All were welcomed with Christian love, with no respect for social, ethnic or political status.

As the church under Constantine's patronage continued to grow it had to pay more attention to administration. In AD 325 the First Council of Nicea made the political province of the empire the basic unit of administration for the church. In 341 the Synod of Antioch moved the divisions even closer to the grass roots. Now bishops were bound to dioceses.

Literally, *diocese* comes from the Greek word *dioikein* which means "to keep house" or "to administer." It was the word chosen by the Roman government for an administrative subdivision. The Council of Antioch defined a diocese as "the whole district which is dependent on a city" (canon 9). The metropolitan of a province was to have authority over all of the bishops in the province (canons 9, 16, 19). Each province was to have two synods (meetings) per year. Church organization was tightening and so was church discipline.

After the Council of Nicea Constantine became less tolerant of different theological points of view. More and more it became important to the church to understand who was catholic, representative of the general, orthodox faith—and who was not.

Deportation and confiscation of places of meeting was the penalty for those who did not hold the faith as it was described first at Nicea and later at Constantinople. Arius and his followers were ordered by Constantine to return to the orthodox church or face a tenfold increase in their pole tax. Arius' books were burned and the discovery of his writings in anyone's home was grounds for capital punishment.

Theodosius was no less energetic in his handling of heretics. Apollinarians, Arians and Macedonians were all under the Emperor's ban. They were not allowed to ordain bishops and the houses where they assembled were to be confiscated. Furthermore, these heretics were to be fined ten pounds of gold. Whereas Constantine had become intolerant of Christian *heretics,* Theodosius rejected *anyone not Christian.*

The Nicene/Constantinopolitan Creed was used as a defensive device, measuring the doctrine of presbyters and bishops. The Creed was not used in worship nor by those seeking baptism. It was a rule of faith to be used by theologians. According to Kelly, "The new creeds" were touchstones by which the doctrines of church leaders might be certified as correct.[94]

For Nicea, and later for Constantinople, *apostolic* meant orthodox and *apostles* meant The Twelve. The doctrine of the faith became more important for the defense of that faith than for mission strategies.

This was especially the case because crowds of new believers began to pack the churches. Everyone was eager to adopt Constantine's religion. It was no longer necessary to convince mission prospects of the superiority of Christianity on the basis of creedal teaching; its preeminence was assumed.

It is not that all creeds had become defensive devices; not at all. With the masses of people pushing to get into church, the clergy became the chief evangelists. Whereas before most were won to the faith by the examples of Christian laity, now most were being brought to Christ through the preaching and teaching of clergy. Creeds were still an integral part of the teaching process.

Epiphanius apparently was not present at the Council of Constantinople; his name is not on the list of participants. But the creed adopted is almost word for word the same as his creed, the baptismal creed of Salamis. In his introduction to this creed Epiphanius had said,

Every person who is in preparation for the holy laver of baptism must learn it [this creed]. They must learn it themselves and teach it expressly, as the one Mother of all of you and of us [the Church] proclaims it …

Around AD 400 Theodore of Mopsuestia wrote a commentary on the Nicene/Constantinopolitan Creed which became a catechism to prepare beginners for baptism. To explain the faith Theodore had preached a series of sermons on the parts of the Creed. The sermons eventually were shaped into chapters of what became Theodore's catechism.

In his commentary on the phrase "And in the Holy Spirit." Theodore tells us why the term was used:

"He [Our Lord] said here also: "In the name of the Father, and of the Son and of the Holy Ghost" in order that his disciples might learn from him that all nations were looking for this name as the cause of all their good things.

And then, in a most mission-minded way, Theodore explained the import of the phrase *he proceeds from the Father*: "Because the Holy Spirit is a Spring which is always with God and has never been separated from him … " and,

He [John] said that the gift of the Holy Spirit will be poured on those who will believe in him, as an undiminished flow of water, because it will be given by God the Spirit, who thus makes manifest his work of giving eternal life to those who believe in him.[95]

Even in the early days of a Christianized Roman Empire there remained a clear association of the phrase *apostolic church* with the third person of the Trinity. This would plead for a missionary emphasis for that phrase: it is the Holy Spirit, continually proceeding from the Father and the Son, who is bringing the Gospel of eternal salvation to all the world. Constantine himself understood that the apostles were the "missionaries to the world."

According to Latourette, Christianity had won the empire by AD 500. A more precise date would be 529. It was at this time that the Emperor Justinian the First closed the ancient schools of philosophy at Athens, an act that symbolized the end of the toleration of the most important rivals of Christianity. For the first 325 years the followers of Jesus had struggled for legitimacy. But in the next 175 years the privileges of state sponsorship brought not only acceptance but success. The Spirit of Christ had triumphed all over the known world. The commission given by Jesus in Matthew 28, if not fulfilled, had been greatly advanced.

Was it only serendipity that the church received the title *apostolic*? I do not think so and wish to ask, "What did God have in mind for this name?" We should not give up too easily on the missionary understanding borne by the title *apostolic*. The gifts God has for us inside of this phrase are the final places to visit and comprise the closing chapters of this journey.

Part V
"One, Holy, Catholic and Missionary"

The Greek word from which our English word *apostolic* descends means "sent." The critical question with which this research has been wrestling is this: "How has the Church been sent?" What can we learn from the church's description as *apostolic* in order to recover a missionary identity for the church today?

The Greek word *apostolos* has changed meanings over the years. At first it referred to a ship, later an export license, a company of colonists, the commander of an expedition and a delegate. For Christians it described a short-term missionary sent out by Jesus, a member of the core leadership group and itinerant missionaries—church planters. Early in church history if someone would have declared that the church was *apostolic* listeners could have understood that to mean, variously, "sent," "missionary" and "authoritative" (true to the teaching of The Twelve).

However, the most helpful question is not what did apostolic mean in the first, second or third centuries—but what meaning can be drawn from this fertile word that will be useful for the church of today?

Chapter 12
Apostolic *Means Sent*

The word *apostle* has had several meanings over the years but basically it has always meant "sent." It is akin to the Latin *mittere* from which the English word missile comes. Early in Christian history *apostle* could have meant Peter or Paul, or one of The Twelve or Silas, Barnabus, Andronicus, Junia or Epaphroditus.

Concerning the word *apostolic,* it might refer to the way in which a church handled doctrine, meaning the content of the faith. The rise of heresy caused the church to limit the final authority for its doctrine and practice to the teaching and example of The Twelve Founder-Apostles. In this dimension the church focuses back, on the original witness; rather than *sent,* it places the emphasis on *kept.*

But there is also a sense in which apostolic can point us ahead, to all who will believe in Jesus; an active not a passive, receptive sense. The "faith of the apostles" is not only understood as the teaching they wrote down, but also the confidence they had—a confidence that moved them to sacrifice, to suffer and die in order to free the Gospel of salvation for all times and to all places. This is the core of the "sentness" of the church; this is the *missionary* emphasis.

The emphasis on *orthodoxy* for the phrase *apostolic church* is a necessary one. But *apostolic church* has other facets, and held up to the light of the Word of God, we can see a missionary emphasis, an emphasis needed today. As Minga observed, "In confessing faith in the Holy Spirit we are confessing faith in a God who is not localized, circumscribed."[96] This is a God who sent "his own son in the likeness of sinful flesh and for sin, he condemned sin in the flesh" (Rom 8:3).

The New Testament apostle was an original—not exactly the same as the Jewish or Gnostic apostles. Credit may be given to Jewish and Gnostic sources, but finally neither fully explains what developed into the kind of missionary we find in the New Testament and first century Christianity.

The Twelve Apostles were interpreters of the tradition but they were also leaders of those sent out on the mission. As such they founded believing communities. Carl Braaten says it well:

Preaching was at the core of their assignment. There were no apostles who were not also missionaries. A church has a right to call itself apostolic only if it carries on the work of the apostles—going into all the world in order to make disciples in all the nations by teaching and baptizing.[97]

We need a more vital understanding of apostolicity, one that will remember its distinctive origins, but which will also impel Christian leaders to reach out to those who are without Christ. Our new day calls for a church that will demonstrate apostolic witness and testimony in its life and work, "for it is through faithful transmission of the preaching and teaching of the apostles that the Church is itself constantly renewed and constituted as Christ's church."[98]

Christ did not enter history once simply to leave a record for all to read and then leave. After the completion of his redemptive work, in triumph he arose from the dead and ascended into heaven to fill all things (Col 1:15-21; 2:9, 10). And he continues to be uniquely present through the means of grace with his church. Jesus' name *Immanuel* still means "God-with-us." This is the dynamic character of the church on earth; its power is not from its history or its truth or even its hope. Christ is its power, its life and its future. In Christ, our sending Lord, the church is still being sent to the lost.

Apostolic church refers to the nature of the church as continuously embodying the mission of the Savior of the world. Jesus was sent on a unique mission: to bear witness to the love of God. This is what the church is sent to do today. This is the *apostolic church.*

It really is not possible, and it certainly is not beneficial, to separate faith content and missionary action in the term *apostolic church.* Both are necessary. It is in this light that we read Acts 4:20, "We cannot help speaking about what we have seen and heard." But as Luther saw new shades of meaning for the phrase *communio sanctorum* in the third article of the Apostles Creed, we can see new shades of meaning in the phrase *apostolic church* in the Nicene Creed, meanings that includes the idea of "sentness"— a unique brand of sentness.

We live in an age of volunteers.

A Lutheran bishop recently told a young people's group the story of his calling into the ministry. One of the children was curious how he had become a bishop, "What courses did you have to take?" How could he prepare, since it was his intention to one day be a bishop? (Contrasted with this is a friend who, after he left his congregation to become the president of a Lutheran Church-Missouri Synod District, was asked by one of his former parishioners how he was doing "now that he had left the ministry"!) No one can choose to become a bishop. God chooses those who will serve in the church.

One did not volunteer to be an apostle; the office was the result of a call. Specifically, a call from God.

It might help to compare the *bishop* and the *shaliach*. The Jewish *shaliach* was not a volunteer: the position was the result of authorization by someone who required representation. This authorization gave the *shaliach* the authority of the sender in one particular area. The one sent did not become the sender but for the specific assignment they carried the full authority of the sender. It was as if the sent one was in fact the sender in that one area of responsibility. If the apostle had been sent to sign a contract for wheat they would not have the authority to buy corn. But any contract signed with authorization of the sender was valid in a court.

Further, there was an urgency to get the job done. The one sent would even be expected to take personal risk, if that is what it would take to accomplish the mission. A bishop such as Ignatius who had been sent to preach the Gospel was not turned back even by threats to his life or property. The mission was urgent and was to be carried out no matter what the cost.

Often the *shaliach* would be asked to move outside of familiar territory to represent the sender. The Jewish apostles regularly worked among synagogues of the diaspora, supervising teaching, collecting contributions for the Jerusalem temple. Their work took them away from their families and friends. The New Testament apostles also left comfort and security to make their way to new coasts where the word of God had not been planted.

How might this compare with a church that aspired to be *apostolic*?

Saying that a church is *apostolic* would mean it had been sent with authority. The authority is the authority of the one by whom the church has been sent. We must not forget that Christ calls and Christ sends the church. The church is founded on the apostles but Christ Jesus is the cornerstone (Eph 2:20). To say the church is *apostolic* is first of all to claim it re-presents Jesus. The church carries Christ's authority to forgive sins.

In John 17:18 Jesus prays for his closest disciples "As you sent [*apesteilas*] me into the world I have sent [*apesteila*] them into the world." And in verse 20 he expands the landscape: "My prayer is not for them alone. I pray also for those who will believe in me through their message." More will be sent to reach others. The sending will continue until the Son is sent one last time.

The Son acted in God's place, and now the Son has authorized the church to act in God's place. In Acts 13 Luke describes "prophets and teachers" of the church in Antioch worshiping and fasting. The Holy Spirit takes over and gives instructions for the worshippers to "set apart Barnabas and Saul for the work to which I have called them" (v. 2). The prophets and teachers then laid hands on them and sent them off.

Their first destination was Salamis, the capital city of Cyprus (where, you will remember, three centuries later Epiphanius, the monk who grew up in Palestine, would teach a baptismal creed that became the forerunner of the Nicene/Constantinopolitan Creed). In the synagogues of Salamis these apostles (Acts 14:14) re-present Christ through the proclamation of his Word. They have been sent by the Holy Spirit; they are not only apostles of the church at Antioch, they are God's apostles. They have been authorized by God.

To say the church is apostolic is to say the church has been sent with authority from God.

And there is an *urgency* to this commission, an urgency that moves an *apostolic* church to take risks to accomplish its assignment.

The disciples braved danger and disappointment because they knew God was with them. After the crucifixion those who had been closest to Jesus were in despair. They took off, left town, or they got out of sight, locking themselves in their hideaway. What brought them back onto the streets, even into the courts of the temple, to face sure arrest and bloody stoning? They had seen Jesus alive! He taught and talked to them. If not for this, the life of Jesus would have been put on a shelf along with all those others who had good intentions but were quickly forgotten when their plans fell apart.

The apostles took risks. They were propelled by the urgency of believing Jesus would return at any moment. This urgency causes the *apostolic* church to sacrifice property, even life, but never the truth and never an opportunity to witness.

This urgency also comes from believing there is only one true God, and all the rest are demons. The apostolic church has a clear understanding of being in an exclusive covenant with the true God. All covenants with other gods lead to death; only this covenant can obtain the guarantee of life.

Well then, how might a church gain this urgency?

In the first place this is God's urgency, mediated through the message of the "apostolic" church. When Peter preached to the Pentecost crowd (Acts 2:14ff) his message produced an immediate desire to change. The response of the listeners was "Brothers, what shall we do?" (Acts 2:37).

The urgency of God working through the apostolic church calls forth an urgency in those who hear the message.

The particular kind of sending enjoyed by the apostolic church is one that moves a church outside of its comfort zone. The Jesus who speaks to the apostles after the resurrection sends them to all the corners of the earth. But what may have been even more difficult for that first church and for the church today is that Christ also sends his messengers to all classes of people.

One day, praying on a rooftop in Joppa, in the afternoon sun, Peter fell into a trance. The last thing he remembered was being hungry and some people making preparations for a meal. The next thing he saw was a huge table-cloth being let down onto the earth. On the cloth were not the usual Jewish foods, but animals that Jews called "unclean" and were prohibited from eat-ing: reptiles, birds and "all kinds of four-footed animals." A voice command-ed him to get up and kill these creatures and eat them. Peter was repulsed by the idea. Three times the message was repeated with an insistent command: "Do not call anything impure that God has made clean." (Acts 10:15)

Apostles went many places with God's message, to the court of the temple, to foreign countries, even to jail. But no apostle was more upset than Peter when he was forced to realize that God also wanted even "those people," gentiles, in his kingdom. Being apostolic means having to leave our places of comfort.

What might be on such a tablecloth if it were to be let down for today's church? People of different races, different ethnic backgrounds—different economic conditions? In some cases this will be as much of a challenge as the one Peter faced. What we must remember is that finally, what is "on the tablecloth" for Christian people is the body and blood of Jesus! In the bread and wine of the eucharist Jesus is with us, still comes to us, to forgive us for our hesitancy to share the Gospel of life with every person, and to give us the strength we need to go into unfamiliar territory.

So far we have looked at three characteristics of an *apostolic* church: a commissioning with authority, a sense of urgency that moves the church to take risks, and a readiness to be uncomfortable for the sake of the proclama-tion. There is at least one more trait we should examine: the *apostolic* church has a particular task it is to accomplish.

The authority, the urgency and the uncomfortableness are not laudable in themselves. They must be in concert with a purpose: to reveal the Good News of salvation through faith in Christ. T.W. Manson said, "The church's essential ministry as the Body of Christ in a real, organic sense, is therefore that of Christ."[99]

In Luke 13 Jesus tells the story of an owner of a vineyard who came to inspect his property. He was particularly intent on finding out why a fig tree planted in the corner of the vineyard had not produced any fruit. In fact, it hadn't produced anything for three years. There was no room in that vineyard for an unproductive plant, and the owner ordered the tree cut out. However, the caretaker interceded on the tree's behalf with a promise to aerate and fer-tilize the soil around it with the hope that next season there would be fruit. If not, then it would be cut down.

Why would there be a fig tree in a vineyard? The obvious and simple response is "to produce." Fig trees are able to grow in soil too poor for grape vines. The parable is told to illustrate the need for repentance; a judgement is coming and all who have not repented will be cut down. As Martin

Scharlemann has pointed out, this parable shows us the patience of God and his anger balanced with each other as at no other place in the Bible. There is, Scharlemann says, "a mysterious line between the two ... "[100]

However, what the parable does not tell us is what happened at the end of the year of grace given to the fig tree. It is not a part of this parable but still we know what happened. We know it was the Owner who was cut down, on behalf of all of us who fail to produce the proper or proper amount of fruit. Christ's death is payment in full.

Yes, we can learn from the apostles what it means to be apostolic, but in the end it is Jesus, *the* Apostle of God, who defines the term. The story of Jesus' life and death for the atonement of sin and his resurrection as victory over the worst Satan can do: this is the important thing. The heart of the apostolic message is that the death and resurrection of Jesus for all people have brought about forgiveness of sins, and therefore eternal life for those who believe. What a message! But the message is useless unless communicated. It is the *apostolic* church as the sent ones of the chief Apostle, Christ, that has been authorized to go with the authority and power of his Word, to offer that forgiveness and hope of life to the world.

This apostolic message is carried by the church into the hearts of those who do not know him. In doing so the apostolic church fulfills the third article of the Nicene Creed. George Forell comments,

> When the Church confesses, "I believe in the Holy Ghost" it acknowledges the sovereign power by which God the Holy Ghost makes "dry bones" into living men and gives new birth to people who are "living dead" because of their estrangement from God.[101]

In love for God and for others the church does many things, but without this one thing (the sense of mission) it is no longer the apostolic church.

Chapter 13
Apostolic or Missionary Church?

Really, it is not correct to put these two adjectives, *apostolic* and *missionary,* in opposition to each other. But that is the point, of this chapter and of this book. And it is the point of the history of many churches.

In the fourth century Christians were exhorted by their bishops not to have contact with pagans. The bishops were concerned that those who affiliated with unbelievers would be affected by their lifestyles. There is nothing new under the sun.

Each year hundreds of churches in the cities of North America shut their doors for the last time. They do so after dwindling to a group too small to maintain basic services. Not in all cases, maybe not even in the majority of cases, but many of these congregations had closed themselves off to the people around them. The mission of the church had become the preservation of the building. Shiny waxed floors and perfectly preserved stained glass windows became victims of steel wrecking balls after a Christian congregation no longer knew how or no longer cared to bring the message of Christ into its neighborhood. Something was essentially wrong in the way it understood its mission, the way it understood *church.*

Peter states this dramatically in 1 Peter 2:9. Speaking to the church he says,

> But you are a chosen people, a royal priesthood, a holy nation, a
> people belonging to God, that you may declare the praises of him
> who called you out of darkness into his wonderful light."

It was not the bishops only, but the whole church, bishops, presbyters, deacons and laity, which was authorized to proclaim God's virtues. The mission is not some disembodied will, it has been given flesh and blood in the women and men baptized into Christ. This flesh and blood is brought to life, animated, by the Spirit. Walter Freytag aptly calls the congregation "the point of breakthrough for the Holy Ghost in the world."

For the church to become apostolic it is necessary for congregations and leaders of congregations to know, in a more profound way, what it means to be missionary. The apostolic congregation reflects in its life the sentness of

God's Christ at the same time as it continues to remember the truth passed down from Christ's apostles. This means several things.

First, it means that commitment to the mission will inform, integrate and lead all the activities engaged in by a congregation seeking to be *apostolic.* Commitment to the mission will permit congregations to set priorities for limited resources of time, talent and money. Evaluation of a congregation's work will be done on the basis of how well it has carried out Christ's mission. All other activities carried on by a congregation will be secondary to the mission enterprise. Bringing the Gospel of Jesus into the world, opening up that point of breakthrough for the Holy Spirit so that lives are changed, is only the essence of congregational work, it is its *raison d'etre,* its reason for being.

Examples abound but one will suffice. It is the natural thing on significant church anniversaries for a congregation to think in terms of a major project. In the past these have tended to be opportunities to increase the commitment of members to the work of the congregation. Often these are times to build the addition, or do major alterations or make repairs to the church building. But not always, and maybe less and less.

In 1986 Ascension Lutheran Church in North Olmstead, Ohio celebrated its last mortgage payment. There had been times in the history of this thirty-five year old congregation when it appeared as if the building would never be paid off! There were some who saw this as a chance to "breathe a little more freely" now that they were out from under a burden that was at times oppressive. Others were anxious to build a gymnasium, to enhance ministry to youth and because "a church needs a debt." For many churches the debt is the only or at least most visible goal they have. But Ascension chose a different path.

Under the guidance of a mission minded leadership, this congregation near Cleveland decided to use the money it had been paying towards its mortgage to begin a new congregation in San Diego. Fifteen thousand dollars a year was pledged by this rust belt congregation to support a full-time mission developer in one of the fastest growing cities in the sun belt.

To be apostolic is to be as committed as God's Apostle Son to carrying out the mission of the Father. The Son is sent as a missionary to the world, to bring the world back to God. The church that is apostolic will follow that same model. The *apostolic church* is the *missionary church.*

St. Patrick writes,

> I heard calling me the voices of those who lived beside the wood of Foclut which is near the western sea, and they cried, "We beg thee, holy youth, to come and walk among us as before."

St. Patrick was born somewhere in Britain, around AD 389. At sixteen he was kidnapped by a band of Irish pirates. Along with many others he was taken to Ireland, where he was forced to be a shepherd in the untamed mountains. After six years he escaped across the Channel to France, but he could never quite forget the people "beside the wood of Foclut." And so somewhere around 432 he went back to Ireland, where the majority of the people were still pagan. In Patrick's description, Ireland was a place "Where never any one had come to baptize, or to ordain clergy or confirm the people."[102]

Patrick was opposed by the pagan priests, by British marauders who constantly interrupted his ministry and killed his converts, and by the Irish kings. But by the time of his death in 461, Ireland was mostly a Christian land. And Irish Christianity was equipped with "an admirable missionary passion."[103]

How can the same passion for mission demonstrated by Patrick become an integral part of the church today? Can it be regained?

It has never been lost. Among individuals, in churches in different parts of our world, in specific congregations, mission is still a burning passion. It is available to fire each congregation and every baptized Christian.

I have tried to show that *apostolic* will be understood with a missionary emphasis when we come into closer contact with the New Testament meaning of the word; when we understand the broader Jewish meaning of the term apostle; when we appreciate the insights of the second and third centuries regarding church growth; and when we discover a broader sense of *apostolic church* in the third article of the Nicene/Constantinopolitan Creed.

Glenn Hinson shares a valuable insight when he contends that no one can succeed either The Twelve or the other eyewitnesses of the resurrection.[104] But there are three things which the church does succeed to in the ministry of the apostles. These three are:

1. the need of the world;
2. the call of Christ; and
3. the tradition of his ministry in the flesh via the body of
   Christ throughout the world.

What the church might do to become *more* apostolic is the subject of the remainder of this chapter.

How can we implement the idea of a *missionary church*? First, by preaching the Gospel. Once again, Carl Braaten:

Apostolicity means doing the apostolic thing, namely, continuing the cause of Jesus .... There is no other way to retain continuity with the apostles than to keep doing what they did— going with the gospel, making disciples of all nations, baptizing them in the name of the Father and of the Son and of the Holy Spirit. That is really all that mission means.[105]

It is imperative that those who occupy the office of the public ministry, the pastors, recognize this. It is imperative because there is no separate missionary office in the church. Instead, the pastoral ministry leads the people of God in missionary service. Primarily the pastor is not a servant to the people, but is a servant to the Word, to Christ himself. "The office which has to proclaim the Word must always keep in mind the expansion of the church."[106]

Second, we can implement the idea of a missionary church by encouraging a mission mind set. It is not a missionary office but a missionary concern that is essential. Christian clergy and lay leaders must awaken and nurture this attitude. In all they do leaders must keep the mission focus. We must become restless in our teaching, not being content to only represent the apostles by maintaining their teachings. We must persuasively re-present Christ to a world that is as unsure of its future as it is of the present.

And all Christians must be more conscious of their involvement in the mission and of the tools God offers to equip us for mission. As baptism makes the new disciple an evangelist, the Lord's Supper is the food for renewal of the mission urgency. So the life of a missionary becomes the life of every member of the body of Christ.

Third, a missionary church would result and the church's work would be more focused if we would pursue the title *missionary* as a proper name for the church. *Apostolic* is not a name that is recognized by most people today; so few know what it means. Confessing faith in an *apostolic* church simply does not communicate the way it once did. *Missionary* communicates.

After a sermon was preached on this subject at First Lutheran Church of Boston the pastor asked the congregation, "Just this one time, as we say the creed, let us say we believe in one, holy, catholic and missionary church." Do you think those people might think differently about their confession of faith when they say the creed again?

The missionary characteristic is in the nature of the church because it is in the nature of God. Through his Holy Spirit God is constantly endowing the church with urgency, always challenging her complacency. God's Spirit moves his people outside of themselves by creating a

> faith that is not passive, dumb, simply contemplative, or selfish, but a faith which produces in the Christian a restless concern for the salvation of others ....[107]

Fourth, a missionary church would result if emphasis were taken off the church as an institution and put on the church as a community of reconciliation. The Christian community has been left on earth for the purpose of reaching those who are without salvation and in-corporating them. But so much time and effort is spent on the corporation.

Many denominations today emphasize starting new churches through existing congregations rather than through a centralized mission board. What is most salutary is the struggle that our faith communities have had when they have had to put their property at risk. I sat through a voters' meeting at my own church in Michigan where we were asking the congregation to allow three unimproved acres of land we own to be used as collateral for a church in Arizona so they could build a first unit.

I watched church council members who had begun this consideration with great skepticism (antipathy?) rise to the occasion as the mission Spirit took over. The more that our members questioned the wisdom of putting our property in jeopardy the stronger became their resolve. These leaders were acutely aware that they had been blessed with so much and now had the God given opportunity to use it so others would come to Christ. And because they were able to communicate this to our members the voters assembly approved the proposal. This certainly is a congregation that deserves the title missionary church.

+   +   +

It is June 26,1991 and my journey is just about over. In the six months that I have been searching for the meaning of the phrase *apostolic church* I have been introduced to many apostles. I have met Jewish apostles and Christian apostles, some of whom I had never known before. And I have become more conscious of the present day apostles, those whom God has allowed to re-present his Son. Especially I have become sensitive to the apostolic church, the living, breathing expanding people of God whom God is sending today as he sent his Son before.

But I must confess that mostly during this time I have come to appreciate more fully *the Apostle*, the Lord of the Church, who travelled further than any missionary ever has or will. Who sacrificed more than I or anyone else ever will. Who loves more than human beings will ever be able to comprehend. Finally, the church belongs to him, and that is why the church is *apostolic*, that is why it will remain *missionary* forever.

Endnotes

1 Forell, George W. *Understanding the Nicene Creed.* Philadelphia: Fortress, 1965. p. 110.
2 Manson, T.W. *The Church's Ministry.* Philadelphia: Westminster, 1948. p. 35.
3 Vicedom, George F. *The Mission of God.* Transl. by Gilbert Thiele and Dennis Hilgendorf. St. Louis: Concordia, 1965. p. 72.
4 Harnack, Adolph von. *The Mission and Expansion of Christianity in the First Three Centuries.* Transl. by James Moffatt. New York: Harper, 1962. p. 11.
5 Vogelstein, Hermann. "The Development of the Apostolate in Judaism and Its Transformation in Christianity" in *Hebrew Union College Annual.* vol. 2, 1925. p. 116.
6 Harnack. p. 329.
7 Manson. p. 43.
8 Scudieri, Robert J. Unpublished poem written for Vacation Bible School at Christ Memorial Lutheran Church, East Brunswick, New Jersey, 1978.
9 Grant, Robert M. *Augustus to Constantine.* San Francisco: Harper, 1990. p. 145.
10 Braaten, Carl E. *The Apostolic Imperative.* Minneapolis: Augsburg, 1985. p. 126.
11 Manson. p. 48.
12 Lightfoot, J.B. *Commentary on the Epistle to the Galatians.* p. 99.
13 Origen. *Commentary on John 13:28.*
14 Rengstorf, Karl Heinrich. "apostello." in *Theological Dictionary of the New Testament.* vol. 1. Ed. by Gerhard Kittel. Grand Rapids: Eerdmans, 1987. p. 399.
15 Schmithals, Walter. *The Office of Apostle in the Early Church.* Nashville: Abingdon, 1969. p. 199.
16 Schmithals. p. 200.

17 *The Apostolic Fathers*. Transl. by J.B. Lightfoot and J.R. Harmer. Ed. and rev. by Michael W. Holmes. Grand Rapids: Baker, 1989. p. 10.

18 Hinson, E. Glenn. *The Evangelization of the Roman Empire*. Macon, GA: Mercer Univ. Pr., 1981. p. 10.

19 Hinson. p. 10.

20 Harnack. p. 11.

21 Harnack. p. 18.

22 Harnack. p. 54.

23 Harnack. p. 70.

24 *The Apostolic Fathers*. p. 4.

25 Fox, Robin Lane. *Pagans and Christians*. New York: Harper, 1987. p. 311.

26 Harnack. p. 22.

27 Latourette, Kenneth Scott. "The First Five Centuries." vol. 1 of *A History of the Expansion of Christianity*. New York, 1937. p. 11.

28 Latourette. p. 16.

29 Grant. p. 85.

30 Grant. p. 264.

31 Grant. p. 174.

32 Fox. p. 269.

33 Fox. p. 269.

34 Grant. p. 172.

35 Grant. p. 173.

36 Fox. p. 268.

37 Harnack. p. 29.

38 Grant. p. 227.

39 Grant. p. 229.

40 Latourette. p. 116.

41 Manson. p. 58.

42 Hinson. p. 10.

43 Hinson. p. 11.

44 Fox. p. 314.

45 Latourette. p. 68.

46 Fox. p. 304.

47 Fox. p. 287.

48 *The Apostolic Fathers*. p. 157.

49 *The Apostolic Fathers*. pp. 155-56.

50 Latourette. p. 116.

51 Hinson. p. 42.

52 Hinson. p. 42.

53 Fox. p. 288.

54 Harnack. p. 49.

55 Grant. p. 258.

56 Grant. p. 259.

57 Harnack. p. 215.

58 Harnack. p. 513.

59 Schaff, Philip. "The History of the Creeds." vol. 1. of *The Creeds of Christendom.* Rev. by David Schaff. Grand Rapids: Baker, 1990. p. 3.

60 Grant. p. 291.

61 Grant. p. 300.

62 Hinson. p. 161.

63 Harnack. p. 349.

64 Burnaby, John. *The Belief of Christendom.* London: S.P.C.K. Publ., 1959. p. 151.

65 Grant. p. 146.

66 Harnack. p. 349.

67 see Clement of Alexandria. *Stromata.* Bk. 4, ch. 17.

68 Latourette. p. 163.

69 Latourette. p. 165.

70 Latourette. p. 68.

71 Fox. p. 613.

72 Fox. p. 615.

73 Fox. p. 616.

74 Fox. p. 236.

75 Grant. p. 245.

76 Fox. p. 625.

77 Grant. p. 239.

78 Latourette. p. 163.

79 Swainson, C.A. *The Nicene and Apostles' Creeds.* London: John Murray, 1875. p. 61.

80 Gray, Crete and Waterhouse. *The Gospel of the Glory of Christ.* London: Epworth, 1946. p. 9.

[81] Lamont, David. *The Church and the Creeds.* London: James Clarke, 1923. pp. 38-40.

[82] Fox. p. 654.

[83] Leitzmann, Hans. "From Constantine To Julian." vol. 3 of *A History of the Early Church.* Cleveland: World, 1964. p. 117.

[84] Leitzmann. p. 117.

[85] Leitzmann. p. 117.

[86] Fox. p. 655.

[87] *The Apostolic Fathers.* p. 144.

[88] *The Apostolic Fathers.* p. 2.

[89] Minga, A. *Commentary of Theodore of Mopsuestia On the Nicene Creed.* vol. 5 of Woodbrooke Studies. Cambridge: W. Heffer, 1932. p. 93.

[90] Kelly, John N.D. *Early Christian Creeds.* 3rd ed. London: Longman, 1972. p. 331.

[91] Leitzmann, Hans. "The Era of the Church Fathers." vol. 4 of *A History of the Early Church.* Cleveland: World, 1964. p. 47.

[92] Schaff. p. 27.

[93] Hinson. p. 15.

[94] Kelly. p. 205.

[95] Minga. p. 109.

[96] Minga. p. 98.

[97] Braaten. p. 125.

[98] Beaver, R. Pierce. "The Apostolate of the Church." in *The Theology of the Christian Mission.* Ed. by Gerald Anderson. New York: McGraw Hill, 1961. p. 287.

[99] Manson. p. 9.

[100] Scharlemann, Martin. *Proclaiming the Parables.* St. Louis: Concordia. pp. 69-70.

[101] Forell. p. 81.

[102] Neill, Stephen. A History of Christian Missions. New York: Penguin, 1987. p. 50.

[103] Neill. p. 50.

[104] Hinson.

[105] Braaten. p. 55.

[106] Vicedom. p. 92.

[107] Vicedom. p. 83.

Index

87